Business
Presen

D0120519

Angela Murray

TEACH YOURSELF BOOKS

For UK order queries: please contact Bookpoint Ltd, 39 Milton Park, Abingdon, Oxon
OX14 4TD. Telephone: (44) 01235 400414, Fax: (44) 01235 400454. Lines are open from
9.00–6.00, Monday to Saturday, with a 24-hour message answering service.
Email address: orders@bookpoint.co.uk

For U.S.A. & Canada order queries: please contact NTC/Contemporary Publishing, 4255
West Touhy Avenue, Lincolnwood, Illinois 60646–1975, U.S.A. Telephone: (847) 679 5500,
Fax: (847) 679 2494.

Long renowned as the authoritative source for self-guided learning – with more than 30
million copies sold worldwide – the *Teach Yourself* series includes over 200 titles in the
fields of languages, crafts, hobbies, and other leisure activities.

British Library Cataloguing in Publication Data
A catalogue entry for this title is available from The British Library.

Library of Congress Catalog Card Number: On file.

First published in UK 1999 by Hodder Headline Plc, 338 Euston Road, London, NW1 3BH.

First published in US 1999 by NTC/Contemporary Publishing, 4255 West Touhy Avenue,
Lincolnwood (Chicago), Illinois 60646–1975, U.S.A.

Typeset by Transet Limited, Coventry, England.
Printed in Great Britain for Hodder & Stoughton Educational, a division of Hodder
Headline Plc, 338 Euston Road, London NW1 3BH by Cox & Wyman Ltd, Reading,
Berkshire.

Impression number   10 9 8 7 6 5 4 3 2 1
Year   2004 2003 2002 2001 2000 1999

CONTENTS

Introduction _____ 1

About this book _____ 1
What is a presentation? _____ 2
Presentation skills in action _____ 3
Believe it or not . . . _____ 4

Section One: Strategies and Skills _____ **5**

**1   A Strategic Approach: Defining the
     Brief** _____ **7**

Why are you giving this presentation? Do you
understand the brief? _____ 7
Understand the hidden agenda _____ 16
Assessing audience knowledge _____ 17
Predict the expectations of your audience _____ 18
Choose your team with care _____ 20
Respect your deadline _____ 21
Strategic planning in practice _____ 22
Summary _____ 24
Do it yourself _____ 25

2   Getting Organized _____ **26**

Appoint a project manager _____ 26
Preparing a planning timetable _____ 27
   Stage one – practical arrangements _____ 27
   Stage two – planning content _____ 33
Planning handout material _____ 36
Rehearsals and practice _____ 38
Professional training _____ 39
Establish a budget _____ 41

Drafting a schedule _____ 41
Planning to meet the impossible deadline!_____ 44
Contingency planning – expecting the unexpected ___ 46
Summary _____ 49
Do it yourself _____ 50

3 Creating a Successful Presentation _____ 51
List the points that must be made_____ 51
Confirm the order of points to be made _____ 53
Creative thinking _____ 54
Adding emphasis – supportive material_____ 57
Copyright _____ 63
Managing and writing content _____ 64
Presenting specific information – managing content
and delivery _____ 69
Planning audience participation _____ 74
Questions and answers_____ 80
Summary _____ 82
Do it yourself _____ 82

4 Communication Skills _____ 83
Remembering your lines _____ 83
Relaxation and dealing with fear _____ 88
Voice control and delivery style_____ 92
Body language _____ 93
Eye contact _____ 95
Communicating as a team _____ 96
Handling question and answer sessions _____ 98
Answering difficult questions _____ 99
Non-verbal communication: personal presentation ___ 101
Personal grooming _____ 106
Colour analysis_____ 107
Creating a presentation wardrobe_____ 108
Summary _____ 109
Do it yourself _____ 110

5 Illustrating Your Presentation _____ 111
Creating visual aids _____ 111
Audio and video clips_____ 114

Presentation software _____ 115
Design and style _____ 116
Presenting information visually _____ 119
Grammar – ensuring consistency _____ 121
Audio-visual equipment – what to use and how
to use it _____ 123
    Flip chart/whiteboard _____ 124
    Portfolio _____ 126
    Overhead projector (OHP) _____ 128
    35 mm slide projector _____ 131
    PC/Multimedia presentation technology ____ 133
Laser pointers _____ 137
CD, Internet and video presentations _____ 138
Practice and training_____ 139
Summary _____ 139
Do it yourself _____ 140

**6 Arrivals, Departures and In Between:
    presentation etiquette _____ 141**
Setting up and settling in _____ 141
Setting up checklist _____ 142
'Before we begin . . .'_____ 144
Planning introductions _____ 145
Remembering names and faces – for you and your
audience _____ 146
When to use handout materials _____ 148
Handout strategies in action _____ 149
Ending a presentation and leaving the venue____ 150
Summary _____ 151
Do it yourself _____ 151

7 Post-presentation Analysis _____ 152
Planning the post-presentation phase _____ 152
Gaining feedback _____ 153
What next? _____ 157
And finally . . . _____ 158
Summary _____ 159
Do it yourself _____ 159

Section Two: Presenter's Checklists _____ **161**

Presenting to an external audience, or one which
has invited you to present_____ 163
Presenting to colleagues, in-house _____ 164
Presenting one-to-one, or to a small group _____ 164
Team presentations_____ 164
Presenting to a large audience _____ 165

Further Reading _____ **166**

Useful Addresses _____ **167**

Index _____ **168**

INTRODUCTION

A recent issue of a men's magazine published a list of the ten most common adult fears. Top of the list was public speaking – ahead of flying (9th), spiders (6th) and even one's own death (which reached joint third place, along with going to the dentist and going out alone at night). Second, by the way, was getting fat.

So if you are reading this book because you find the thought of presenting daunting, nerve-wracking and frankly frightening, don't worry – you're not alone!

In many industries, presentations are a fact of business life. Presenting ideas to clients or colleagues, pitching for new business, launching a new product – in any situation where a message needs to be communicated, a presentation may be the most appropriate method. And not all presentations need be formal, sit down affairs. Outlining a new idea to your boss; showing your portfolio to a prospective client in the reception of their office block; discussing ideas with colleagues; explaining office procedure to new recruits. These could all be described as presentations.

Being able to deliver an effective presentation often plays a part in career development, demonstrating skills on a number of levels. The ability to structure a coherent script, to speak in front of an audience (who may not always be on your side), to manage a number of different resources in order to meet a deadline on time, and to think on your feet and act with confidence, for example.

About this book

Teach Yourself Business Presentations provides an overview of those skills and techniques which will prove most useful in a presentation and is an ideal starting point for anyone with limited practical experience who would like to know more. It's likely that you work in a small to medium-sized business where presentations are a regular, but not everyday, activity – but even if you are a practised presenter I hope this book will prove useful, stimulating new ideas, or simply providing reassurance that your current technique is still valid and effective.

As I've already indicated, a presentation can focus on almost any aspect of your business and so it's impossible to be too specific about *content*. Instead, the book will focus on effective planning, creative thinking, successful delivery and meaningful evaluation. Many of the hints and tips given are neither new nor revolutionary: instead, they summarize tried and tested techniques. Exactly what the nervous presenter needs when starting out.

Teach Yourself Business Presentations is divided into two sections. The first, main, section takes you through the various stages involved in creating a successful presentation, and looks at the necessary skills needed. The second section takes the viewpoint of someone planning a more specific presentation, drawing together information to provide a useful set of checklists and summaries. In this way, I hope the book will act both as a teacher, helping you hone your presentation skills ready for the next big occasion, and as a handy reference guide, to help you check that your planning has been as thorough as possible.

What is a presentation?

Presentations can take many forms but they all have one thing in common: on one side there is a presenter (or team); on the other there is the audience, which can range from a single individual to a theatre packed to the roof. The audience is there to listen to the presentation and consider the subject matter being presented. And so, whatever the scenario, the presenter must be clear and effective, and the audience must leave having understood the aim of the presentation. Neither must feel that the whole experience was a waste of valuable time.

Every presentation is different – in its aims, in its context, in the nature of the audience, and in the expected outcome. In essence, every presentation has its own unique set of dynamics and it's your job to pin these down and establish how to respond in your planning and delivery.

As a general rule of thumb, however, presentations can be grouped into three categories:

■ **Persuasive**

Aiming to influence the behaviour of the audience in some way. This category embraces credentials presentations, new business pitches, sales presentations and product launches, and presentations at which the speaker is challenging an established viewpoint.

■ **Informative**

Presenting factual information: explaining health and safety procedures to new recruits for example, or reporting on the performance of a department to members of the board. Although the presentation will be factual, it's not always the case that subsequent question and answer sessions or discussions will also be as straightforward. The presenter may also have to be persuasive to make sure some of the points made are fully understood.

■ **Instructive**

The next step on from the informative presentation, as the audience will be expecting to gain new knowledge or information *and* the ability to use it. Most training presentations can be classed as 'instructive' – but this book is not aimed at the professional trainer, or for those who have to deliver fully structured training courses. We'll be looking at one-off situations where a presenter needs to explain a technique or skill in some detail.

Presentation skills in action

As you work your way through this book you'll find many different examples used to illustrate the points made, but to help put some of the skills into practice we'll look at three specific scenarios, each illustrating one of the categories identified above:

Marvellous Marketing – the persuasive team presentation

Marvellous Marketing, a marketing agency, has been invited to present its ideas for a marketing strategy to a local firm, in order to try to win a major contract. The presentation is a team effort, and will also be a competitive exercise. Other marketing firms are also presenting, each trying to win the business – this is sometimes called a 'beauty contest'.

Crazy Crackers Ltd – the informative presentation

The Personnel Department has asked Bill Bailey, Financial Director, to give the company's latest new recruits an introduction to the Accounts Department. He's drafted in Sarah Williams, who works as a manager in the department, to help him.

Information for Business – the instructive presentation

Tom Collins runs a small consultancy which advises companies on how to make the most of IT. He's been asked to give a presentation to members of a Business Club on 'Using the Internet for Business' – it's one of a series of evening presentations given by the Club, which aims to provide practical advice and help on a particular topic. Tom will have to deliver an instructive presentation which may comprise a number of sections, all strung together coherently. His audience has also paid for the privilege of listening to him.

These three scenarios will help you understand how theory works in practice. Your presentation will be different from all the examples quoted in this book, but you'll see how to adapt and tailor the advice to suit your own situation.

Believe it or not . . .

A final point. Believe it or not, some people actually enjoy presenting – their blood races, their heart pumps and they feel a thrill akin to that of an actor going on stage. With enough practice, and armed with enough knowledge, you might find that you enjoy presenting as well!

Section One

STRATEGIES AND SKILLS

1 | A STRATEGIC APPROACH: DEFINING THE BRIEF

When starting to plan a presentation, it's very important to stop and take a *strategic* look at what you are about to do. Identifying, in advance, the broad context surrounding your presentation will influence all the subsequent decisions you will have to make, saving time and ensuring the end result is as effective as possible.

So, how to start strategic planning – and get it right? Let's begin with the most fundamental question:

Why are you giving this presentation? Do you understand the brief?

If you've been *asked* to give a presentation, then you'll have been given a brief – summarized instructions – asking you to present. (If the decision to present is yours alone read this section first, but also see the later section entitled 'Writing a brief for yourself'.)

The nature of the brief reflects the nature of the presentation. Let's take a look at the brief given to the team at Marvellous Marketing. One day, they receive a letter from one of the town's biggest employers . . .

Jane Smith	Industrial Instruments Ltd
Senior Consultant	River Park
Marvellous Marketing	Old Town
High Street	
Old Town	2 February xxx1

Dear Ms Smith

We are currently reviewing our marketing strategy and budgets, and have identified a need for an external resource to support next year's marketing campaign and our export drive in particular. We are currently looking at a number of agencies which could provide such support, and I would therefore like to invite Marvellous Marketing to present to our board of directors on Tuesday, 3 March at 11.15, at the Old Bridge Hotel, River Street, Old Town. I would be grateful if you could confirm your attendance with my personal assistant, Linda Evans, as soon as possible.

We would like your presentation to cover not only your company and its experience, but also what it could do for Industrial Instruments in the overseas arena. We would like to meet the members of your organization who would be working with us, if you were awarded the contract. We have allocated one hour for your presentation.

I am sure you will need further information on Industrial Instruments and our objectives: please contact Linda to make an appointment to meet, when I will be happy to brief you further.

Yours sincerely

Arthur Jones
Marketing Director

As you can see, this brief is highly formal and carefully structured. But a brief can also be very informal: a memo, a chat in the corridor or a message on an answer-phone, perhaps. Let's see how our second presentation team receives their call to action:

(A voice mail message for Bill Bailey, Financial Director, Crazy Crackers, from Leslie Rogers, Head of Personnel, Tuesday 3 February)

Bill, it's Leslie from Personnel here. We're giving the latest new recruits a formal tour of the offices and factory next Tuesday morning (the 10th) – you know, the usual stuff. I've booked a slot in your diary for 9.30 – could you give them the potted company history and a run-down of the Accounts Department? I'll pick them up afterwards and take them round the building. Thanks

---

Let's look at one more brief, given to Tom Collins over at Information for Business. As in many 'instructive' presentations, the presenter, organizer and audience are on more equal terms, even though the brief is couched in quite a formal style.

Tom Collins
Managing Director
Information for Business
Unit 11a
Phoenix Business Park
Old Town

Helen Johnson
Chair
Old Town Business Club
Meander House
Long Lane
Old Town

1 September xxx1

Dear Tom

It was good to see you again last week, and I was delighted to hear that your new business venture is proving a success. Further to our discussion, on behalf of the Old Town Business Club I would like to invite you to take part in our ongoing programme of evening presentations, to talk on 'Using the Internet for Business'.

We promote these presentations very much as practical events, at which the audience can expect to receive information relevant to their business, and even to practise new skills which they can implement in their daily work. As you may know, previous courses have included 'Managing paperwork for export', 'An introduction to marketing for the small business', and 'Employers' rights and responsibilities – a beginners' guide'. We limit places to 20, and all presentations are held in the training room here at Meander House. If demand is high, we may ask you to give the presentation more than once.

Currently we have two dates free: 27 January or 11 February. The presentations run from 7 pm until 9.30 pm, and are preceded by a light buffet which starts at 6.30 pm. A break is also included halfway through. Although we do not pay a fee as such, we will cover any reasonable expenses, and, of course, the presentation would provide a very good opportunity to promote your company to all the members of the Old Town Business Club.

I do hope you are interested in our suggestion. Please let me know as soon as possible which is the more convenient date, and also provide a brief synopsis of the presentation which we can use in our publicity material. We can arrange to discuss your presentation in more detail nearer the time.

Yours sincerely

Helen Johnson

Confirming the brief – a basic checklist

Once you've received a brief it's a very good idea to rewrite it in your own words and then copy it back to the person who asked you. This will ensure your understanding of their request, and also demonstrate your commitment to getting it right. It's also very important, at this early stage, to make sure you have enough information to start planning: if not, you can include this request in your response.

To confirm a brief thoroughly, work through a basic list of all the facts you need to check, divided into two essential categories: firstly the aims of the presentation. You need to confirm:

> the goal of the presentation
>
> what the audience will be expecting to see and hear (to ensure core subject matter and key points are agreed in advance, and that the general approach is correct)
>
> ■ the level and range of audience knowledge on the subject in question (so that you can pitch the presentation correctly)
>
> ■ an estimate of audience size
>
> the proposed structure and timing of the presentation.

And secondly the practical arrangements:

> ■ venue
>
> ■ date
>
> time
>
> the name(s) of the presenter or presentation team
>
> ■ organizational responsibilities (i.e. who is in charge of booking or arranging the venue)
>
> time of arrival, if ahead of the presentation
>
> an indication of the visual aids which you can use or the equipment which will be available to you (this often depends upon the venue).

You may find that you have more questions than answers at this stage (which is probably a good sign), so don't be afraid to get back in touch with whoever gave you the brief to work through any details that seem unclear. Not all details need to be pinned down precisely, but you need enough information to begin planning with some degree of accuracy.

To give you an idea, here are the responses to the briefs we've already looked at. Jane Smith at Marvellous Marketing is responding in two stages – first to Arthur Jones at Industrial Instruments, and secondly to his PA, to confirm practical details.

Arthur Jones
Marketing Director
Industrial Instruments Ltd
River Park
Old Town

Jane Smith
Senior Consultant
Marvellous Marketing
High Street
Old Town

2 February xxx1

Dear Mr Jones

Thank you very much for your letter of 2 February, inviting Marvellous Marketing to present to the board of Industrial Instruments Ltd on 3 March at 11.15 am. I have already confirmed with Linda that we are able to attend.

Presenting with me will be Pauline Palmer, Managing Director of Marvellous Markting, and Fergus Davis, Consultant, who is our export specialist.

In our presentation, we will give a brief history of Marvellous Marketing (as we appreciate that not all members of your board will be familiar with our company), its capabilities and experience, and then examine in more detail the needs of your export division and how we will be able to help maximize current promotional activities for the forthcoming campaign. This main section of our presentation should take around 40 minutes, leaving 20 minutes for further discussion, questions and answers.

We would very much like to meet you, as you suggested, ahead of the presentation to obtain a more in-depth brief, in order to ensure that our presentation – and our accompanying proposal document – meet the expectations of Industrial Instruments Ltd. I will contact Linda to arrange a time to meet.

Thank you once again for giving us this opportunity to present to you, and we look forward to meeting you in due course.

Yours sincerely

Jane Smith
Senior Consultant

Linda Evans
PA
Industrial Instruments Ltd
River Park
Old Town

Marvellous Marketing
High Street
Old Town

2 February xxx1

Dear Linda

Further to our conversation yesterday, I am writing to confirm our attendance at the presentation on 3 March, at the Old Bridge Hotel, at 11.15. We would like to use the OHP facilities provided by the Hotel, and we will need about 15 minutes to set up before we begin our presentation.

I understand from Mr Jones that he expects around 11 people to attend the presentation – is it possible to have their names in advance, so that we can personalize any handout material we prepare?

I look forward to speaking to you again soon.

Yours sincerely

Jane Smith

How does Bill Bailey respond to the message left on his telephone?

MEMO
From: Bill Bailey, Finance
To: Leslie Rogers, Personnel
cc: Sarah Williams, Accounts
Re: Presentation to new recruits

Thanks for your message. Just to let you know, Sarah's booked the large meeting room for 9.30 on Tuesday 10 February, as I gather there will be about ten people taking the tour – please could you confirm this. As we are the first stop on their tour, should we arrange refreshments? I'll give them the standard company slide show if that's OK (it lasts about 30 minutes) and then Sarah will take them through the workings of the Accounts Department: probably just a quick chat and a handout listing names and job titles. Sarah will sort the room out in advance. The whole presentation should only take about 45 minutes – depending on how many questions they ask – so do you want to come and pick them up at 10.15?

Note that even though the brief was little more than a conversation, Bill is careful to put his response in writing. This makes sure everyone has a written record to refer to.

Finally, let's look at Tom Collins' response to Helen Johnson's letter. As we know, Tom has a lot more time to play with when planning his presentation, and so confirmation of precise details can be left until later. However, Tom is already thinking ahead about the practical implications of his presentation, and wants to flag them up at this early stage:

Helen Johnson   ·   Information for Business
Chair   Unit 11a
Old Town Business Club   Phoenix Business Park
Meander House   Old Town
Long Lane
Old Town   3 September xxx1

Dear Helen

Thank you for your letter and your invitation to present to the Old Town Business Club. I would be delighted to host a presentation on 'Using the Internet for Business', and the most convenient date would be 27 January.

I will gladly forward a synopsis of the presentation I could give, but I first need to confirm the following details. I will need to use at least three or four networked computers (controlled by the presenter's PC), which are linked to the Internet. Will the Meander House Training Room be suitable for such a set-up? As you suggested, I would like to meet nearer the time to go through the details of the presentation but I thought it wise to discuss the venue at this point, just in case you need to arrange and advertise a different venue to your members.

Thank you very much for asking me to take part in your programme of events, and I look forward to speaking to you again very soon.

Yours sincerely

Tom Collins

In summary, the response can be as formal or as informal as the brief. Its main purpose is to ensure that you have understood exactly what is required of you, have highlighted any details that are unclear, anything you don't know and made arrangements to obtain the relevant information, and so can begin detailed planning in confidence.

Writing a brief for yourself

If you've initiated the presentation, start by writing your own brief along the lines recommended above. It's easier than you think to forget crucial details (such as booking the venue!) when your mind is focused on what you are going to say and how you are going to say it.

It's a good idea to run your brief past colleagues or superiors (and, if possible, a sample from your target audience) at this early stage. A presentation is a demanding activity – demanding of your efforts and presentation skills, and of the time and attention of your audience. It's important to ensure that your audience considers the presentation to be a good idea before you start your preparations – you don't want them to feel resentful before you've even begun to speak.

Circulate the brief

Once the brief is accepted and confirmed, copy it to all parties involved in the preparations – your superior for example, who has sanctioned the activity, and any administrative staff who will be needed. You need to make sure that everyone knows that the presentation is on the horizon and that they need to clear space and time for any necessary actions, no matter how small their ultimate involvement may be.

You've considered the brief – do you still want to present?

An important point. Once you've examined the brief in detail, you may conclude that a presentation is not the best response. There might be a number of reasons for this:

- The subject matter is too specific for any but the smallest group and a discussion meeting would be more appropriate.
- If the subject matter is highly complex, a presentation may result in unnecessary simplification. The information may be better presented in written form, where readers can have

access to both summary and technical details simultaneously, and can read it thoroughly at their leisure.

- Practical details stand in your way. It's impossible to find a place and time suitable for all interested parties, or the right speakers are simply unavailable on the right day. Postponement is a good alternative to complete cancellation, unless the presentation has to be delivered by a certain date. Perhaps a video, CD or Internet presentation might be a practical solution? (See Chapter 5 for more on these.)

- You may judge the time (and possibly money) spent in preparation does not justify even the best possible outcome, especially if you have to travel some distance to present. Perhaps the straightforward circulation or posting on of relevant information would be just as effective? Or is there a hidden agenda at work (and we'll look at hidden agendas in the next section)? If you often present in order to win business, you may sometimes suspect you're being asked to present for all the wrong reasons – as an opportunity to pick your brains for free, or to provide a benchmark against which to judge a current incumbent supplier (and you're being used to make a current supplier drop his fees). Alternatively, do you really want the work or contract that is on offer? It takes courage to turn down the chance to win business, but such a decision is justified if the expense and exhaustion of planning and preparation aren't worth the final outcome.

Understand the hidden agenda

Once the 'official' brief is confirmed, clarify, in your mind, any hidden agendas influencing your presentation. Consider the following:

- Is the presentation a test of personal skills, prior to possible promotion or as on-the-job training? If so, you'll need to meet the expectations of both your audience and those judging your performance.

- Will the success of your presentation reflect upon a superior, justifying his or her decision to ask you to present? What can you do to make sure you don't let him or her down?

- How important is this presentation to your business? Are you presenting in order to win business or as a PR exercise? What are the short- and long-term gains you hope your presentation to achieve?
- Are some members of the audience likely to be unsupportive? Who are they and why? What can you do to turn everyone in the same direction?
- Are you having to act as a messenger for something beyond your personal remit – perhaps explaining a business decision that might result in redundancies or announcing poor profits. Why were *you* asked to deliver the bad news? How do you emerge from such a presentation with your own reputation intact?

Analyzing hidden agendas is not an exercise in cynicism, or an encouragement to develop intricate conspiracy theories. It's simply that a presentation can work on many different levels: by identifying these levels you can prepare for any implications they might have.

Assessing audience knowledge

An important part of confirming the brief is to establish the level of understanding that your audience will have, and you can find this out in a variety of ways. If you are presenting 'out of house' then talk to your contact at the host organization; alternatively talk to members of your prospective audience or circulate a questionnaire in advance. You can even restrict your audience by only allowing those with a certain level of knowledge to attend.

It might be the case that you can predict what your audience will be like without any detailed research. Marvellous Marketing, for example, is presenting to board members, and the team knows that some will understand marketing strategy, but others will know nothing, yet are still very important members of the group they hope to impress. Rather than focus on detailed marketing techniques, Marvellous Marketing will concentrate on how these translate into business benefits, and the reasons why they should implement them. They can detail the actual activities they propose in an accompanying document for all to read.

Bill Bailey and Sarah Williams are also on easy ground: they know the audience will know nothing, and so can prepare their material with confidence. Tom Collins will not be so sure: he's considering sending delegates a questionnaire in advance, so he can judge their level of technical ability. Alternatively, he may suggest that the presentation is more appropriate for those with a certain basic level of knowledge.

Predict the expectations of your audience

The next stage in your strategic planning is to try to predict the *expectations* of your audience and its mood on the day of your presentation – a separate exercise from deciding what information they want or are expecting to hear.

Establishing the mood of your audience is essential when trying to set the pitch of your presentation: its informality, its style and appearance. The audience you face is not always supportive and receptive. The audience could be:

- hostile and uncommunicative, waiting to tackle you on any number of issues and unconcerned if you are shot down in flames (consider the atmosphere if you had to present poor performance figures to your superiors or to your clients)
- open-minded but waiting to be convinced – perhaps you're selling something, and they want to know why they should buy it
- inherently interested, supportive and encouraging, eager to hear what you have to say and ready to contribute to your main points
- sceptical, feeling they are under duress by having to attend at all
- bored – perhaps you have to talk about a rather dull subject
- highly attentive and unlikely to let any mistakes go unchallenged – particularly if your audience has paid money to attend. They will demand the results promised.

How do you plan for such a range of moods?

Define your tactics

For each type of audience outlined above, we can start to sketch out a tactical response: in practice you may find your audience is a mixture of the categories listed above, but it's useful to start with a few basic generalizations. As you proceed through this book, you'll be able to flesh out these tactical responses further. Let's start by grouping our categories together into similar types:

The hostile and uncommunicative audience

As they say, 'you've got to accentuate the positive'! Positive words, positive body language, even positive clothes. Team presentations can bolster confidence in such situations, especially if one team member is specifically chosen for seniority, gravitas or personal presence. If this isn't possible, then enlist colleagues for moral support and expert input as required, especially during question and answer sessions.

The reserved or sceptical audience, waiting or wanting to be convinced

This audience will expect both a positive *and* persuasive presentation, one which is both convincing and which creates an atmosphere of trust. Background research into your audience may highlight topics or presentation styles that should be avoided at all costs, or that may touch buttons and win respect.

The supportive audience, eager to contribute and discuss

This needs a presentation that is fairly fluid and adaptable, and which includes plenty of opportunity for carefully managed audience participation. Even though you'll want to encourage audience interaction, checks and balances will still be needed to keep the proceedings under control. The presenter will need a certain 'stage presence' to manage interruptions effectively and courteously: a basic timetable, handed out at the start of the presentation, will help structure proceedings and enable you to spend the right amount of time on each point.

The bored, listless audience

You've drawn a short straw, so how do you make it a long one? Base your presentation around surprise, interaction and enjoyment – no matter how dull the subject matter may be. Keep the presentation short, and the audience on its toes. Many ideas for enlivening a presentation are included in this book.

A number of the tactics listed above are interchangeable and your final plan will depend entirely upon the specific circumstances at play in your own situation. Good tactical planning demands a broad knowledge of presentation techniques and skills, which the following chapters in this book will supply. But even at this early stage, you can see how the most basic planning, combined with simple common sense, can shape and guide your subsequent preparations, steering you in the right direction from the beginning.

Choose your team with care

If you are presenting as a team then once you've run through all these strategic issues, it's time to select those individuals who can meet the demands of the presentation – if you have the luxury of choice of course. If you can't pick and choose, then home in on those skills and character types best suited to the presentation and audience, and make sure each team member knows which elements of his or her own personality to exploit.

Ideally, every presenter should combine knowledge and experience of the subject matter with presentation skills appropriate to the situation, and be able to create the right 'chemistry' with the audience – in a team presentation you can split those skills between a number of individuals. For example, will your presentation cover technical or financial issues? Then make sure your team includes someone with relevant expertise who can answer more detailed questions. Is the presentation to be a multi-media event? Then you must include someone capable of handling the software and hardware involved. Will your audience expect to see a senior member of your organization present? Senior staff need not even take part in the presentation, but can still act as 'host' if that is what the audience expects.

Which brings us on to the selection of the presentation leader – a vital figure in a group, as the leader will be the main reference point for the audience, introducing, leading and concluding the event. When selecting this individual, you'll want to establish him or her as an authority figure, but remember that authority can come in a number of different ways:

- formal – in essence, managerial
- advisory – if the individual is the leading expert in that particular field
- charismatic – simply good at delivering engaging presentations
- budgetary – important if your presentation has financial implications.

Choose your leader carefully, and make sure he or she meets the expectations and mood of the audience. An audience wanting to be instructed will want an expert not a manager; an audience worried about business developments will want a manager not a PR person who is excellent at presenting.

And one final point. If possible try not to field a presentation team larger than your audience – it can prove very intimidating!

Respect your deadline

And don't try to be too ambitious! After analyzing the brief, you may feel the presentation deadline is unrealistic: the brief demands a lot of information that has yet to be researched, for example, or a level of technical sophistication that cannot be delivered at the drop of a hat. If this is the case, try to negotiate a later date as soon as you can. Presenting is a stressful business at the best of times, without adding unnecessary pressure! If changing the deadline proves impossible your planning will have to be all the more meticulous, and extra resources mustered as quickly as possible. Later in this book we'll examine some basic project management techniques and 'forward planning' suggestions which can help you prepare for even the most unrealistic deadline.

Strategic planning in practice

Let's return to the main issue this chapter aims to address – strategic planning. To summarize, the strategic plan aims to establish:

- goals and objectives of the presentation for both you and your audience
- basic practical details
- expectations of your audience
- hidden agendas at work
- tactical responses.

There's no need to prepare complex plans and documents at this stage – after all you have better things to spend your time on now – but just note down the factors that have to be considered in order to shape the next planning stage.

So how are our presenters doing? Let's look at the strategic plans that underpin two of our teams' preparations – and leave the third to you!

Jane Smith, at Marvellous Marketing, has been assigned the role of project leader for the presentation (and we'll look more closely at project management in the next chapter). One of her first actions is to put her strategic plan in writing and copy it to her co-presenters.

As you can see, Jane chooses to do this in a memo, rather than prepare a formal action plan, as she doesn't want to waste valuable time at this stage on 'plans for plans'. Putting down your strategic thoughts as a memo, email or even recorded in the minutes of your first formal planning meeting will all work equally well. The most important objective is to commit those strategic thoughts to paper, to ensure everyone involved in the presentation can refer back to the same information as they fulfil their individual tasks.

MEMO

From: Jane
To: Pauline, Fergus
Re: Presentation to Industrial Instruments Ltd

As you all know we have been asked to present to Industrial Instruments Ltd on 3 March at 11.15 am: this is a very important presentation for us, so could I make the following points before we start detailed planning:

■ The brief has been confirmed by exchange of letters, but we need more information on the company's main target markets and financial goals, etc., as well as its likely budget. Fergus and I are to meet the Marketing and Export Directors next week to obtain this information. I'm handling all the practical details, so all queries come through me.

■ This presentation is very important for Marvellous Marketing: it's potentially a very large contract and would strengthen our client list considerably. We need to devote serious resources of time (and possibly money) to getting it right.

■ The focus is clearly on international marketing, therefore we all need to think of relevant examples to include in the presentation and proposal, and in any work samples or handouts.

■ This is a competitive pitch – I will try to find out who we are presenting against, but I suggest we identify our strengths and weaknesses with regard to the brief (and our competitors) as soon as we can, and build the results into our presentation. Whatever we do, we must emphasize our experience in marketing, especially in export marketing, and our value for money.

■ We're presenting to the Board so expect a detailed understanding of the instrumentation industry but a very varied understanding of marketing techniques – we need to research the international instrumentation industry asap.

■ We have a month to prepare but we must not become complacent – this presentation must become one of our top priorities.

Over at Crazy Crackers Ltd, Sarah Williams has just left a meeting with Bill Bailey, the Finance Director. Here are her notes:

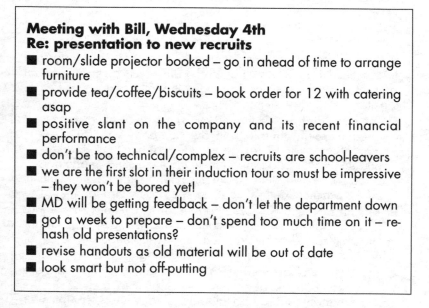

Meeting with Bill, Wednesday 4th
Re: presentation to new recruits
- room/slide projector booked – go in ahead of time to arrange furniture
- provide tea/coffee/biscuits – book order for 12 with catering asap
- positive slant on the company and its recent financial performance
- don't be too technical/complex – recruits are school-leavers
- we are the first slot in their induction tour so must be impressive – they won't be bored yet!
- MD will be getting feedback – don't let the department down
- got a week to prepare – don't spend too much time on it – re-hash old presentations?
- revise handouts as old material will be out of date
- look smart but not off-putting

Summary

- Strategic planning helps shape your presentation, and lays the foundation for effective practical planning.
- Understand the reasons why you are presenting – and confirm your understanding with everyone involved.
- Try to identify and appreciate any hidden agendas at work.
- Try to assess your audience: the information it wants to hear, how much it already knows, its mood on the day and how this will impact upon your presentation.
- Define the tactics you'll need to meet and/or counter audience expectations.
- If presenting as a team, choose your co-presenters with care.
- Respect your deadline.

Do it yourself

Now it's your turn! Taking Tom Collins's presentation for the Old Town Business Club as your guide, sketch out a basic strategic plan for him to use. Don't forget:

■ Has the brief been confirmed?
■ What are the practical details?
■ Do you think Tom has enough information on which to plan his presentation?
■ How can he define his audience and its expectations?
■ How important is this presentation for his company?
■ What tactics should he consider as he starts to prepare?
■ How much time has he got to prepare?

2 | GETTING ORGANIZED

A successful presentation depends upon faultless organization. And much of this revolves around the checking and double-checking of all the many and varied components which go to make up the presentation you deliver. This chapter covers the basic planning needed when putting a presentation together, and I've assumed that you have a reasonable amount of time in which to prepare. But you won't always be so lucky! Don't worry if the level of detail described seems daunting. You probably won't need to do all the actions recommended for each presentation you give: and at the end of the chapter we'll look at ways of adapting the advice given to suit a far shorter timeframe.

Appoint a project manager

A first step in the planning phase is to identify a 'project manager' for the presentation. If you are the only person closely involved, then this is a rather academic exercise. But if the presentation is a team effort, and involves the complex planning of content and delivery, then choosing the right person for the job is very important. A project leader must have good organizational and time management skills, and have an ability to pay attention to detail whilst keeping an eye on the broader picture. Most important of all will be the ability to delegate effectively and to manage the team of helpers recruited to assist in the preparation and planning phase, and to arbitrate when views differ.

In team presentations the project manager, although a key member of the presentation team, need not necessarily be the 'leader' of the presentation when delivered, or the most senior person: in fact, it's often wiser to delegate the planning to someone with less on their plate than a senior colleague.

So congratulations! You've been selected to manage the planning of your presentation. If you are facing this mountain alone, and can foresee the need for additional assistance, enlist this help now and give your aides a full briefing on the presentation in hand and what needs to be done to prepare for it. Most importantly, make sure they have the time available to help you when you need it most.

Preparing a planning timetable

Bringing basic project management skills to presentation planning will simplify the procedure for all involved, and will help clarify responsibilities right from the start. In essence, your aim is to identify the following:

■ The tasks which must be completed in order to be ready on time.

■ The length of time each task will take.

■ Those tasks which can run in parallel without impeding the progress of the whole project.

■ The deadline for each task.

■ The 'milestones' – those times when control leaves your hands (for example, when you have to hand the text for visual aids over to an external designer).

■ Individuals responsible for each task, and especially for monitoring milestones.

■ The times when extra assistance will be needed, for which tasks and for how long.

Your first objective is to identify which tasks will take longest to complete, and those details which need to be confirmed as soon as possible. Work on these tasks as soon as you can but don't be tempted to delegate too quickly. You may ending up wasting time needlessly unless you've really thought through what has to be done.

So what do you actually need to consider when preparing your list of tasks? Let's look at a basic checklist, which goes over – in more detail – the points we confirmed at the brief. To make life even easier, let's group the checklist into two basic stages:

Stage one – practical arrangements

Double-check date, time, venue and audience

Ideally this is confirmed when the brief is 'accepted', but sometimes presentation venues have yet to be decided when the green light is given, or else the responsibility for finding a venue is given as part of your brief.

Confirming the venue is among the top priorities. If you are presenting in-house, ensure the room you want is booked as soon as the date is confirmed. If you have to book a room elsewhere run through the checklist later on in this section to make sure it meets your basic criteria and then confirm your booking. If you have been asked to present in a venue managed by someone else, simply confirm in writing what you understand to be the arrangements, as we discussed in Chapter 1. A follow-up phone call nearer the time to double-check details will also help ensure everything stays on course, and – if scheduled properly – will give you enough time to make alternative arrangements if things don't go to plan.

If you have initiated the presentation, then it may also be your responsibility to ensure that the audience knows of the date and place well in advance, and you may even need to allow time to find a date and place suitable for all concerned.

If you are invited to present, then your audience will take care of itself, although it is important to know from the outset (as we discussed in the first chapter) how many people will be in the audience. Again, double-check this detail nearer the time to allow you to prepare for last minute changes.

Confirm presenters and assistants: book key meetings into diaries

It would be foolish to confirm a date and time if the presenter couldn't make it! But although this process should be automatic, don't forget to put the presentation into the diaries of everyone concerned as soon as possible. You'll need to tell:

- Other members of the presentation team, or colleagues you might like to attend the presentation in order to give moral support or to provide expert input (remember our tactical plan).
- Colleagues who should attend key planning meetings or could contribute to brainstorming sessions.
- Colleagues who can review draft scripts and watch rehearsals.

■ In-house services which may be needed: secretarial or administrative support; in-house designers, caterers or other services.

Confirm in writing the commitment you expect from your team, and make sure they have all earmarked the necessary time to complete any jobs they have promised to help you with – and if they can't then find someone else straight away.

Don't forget an understudy

If you know that your presentation would be impossible to postpone or rearrange at short notice (you're taking part in a competitive pitch, for example, or in a widely advertised event) then ask a colleague to act as an understudy. Even the most conscientious individual can suddenly fall ill – and although you may think that adrenalin will get you through, your audience may not want to listen to someone who should clearly be in bed!

If you are presenting as a team then another team member can step into your shoes, but you may still need extra backup to fill that vacant seat. If you are presenting alone, ask someone with lots of presenting experience to act as your potential stand-in, as he or she will have the confidence to step in at the last moment and handle any mistakes in a professional manner.

Assess the venue

The room in which you present will greatly influence:

■ The choice of AV techniques open to you.

■ The audience's impression of you and your organization (especially if you have selected the venue).

■ The formality or informality of the presentation and the comfort or otherwise of your audience.

As you can see, it's very important to assess your venue, critically, as soon as you can, in order to address any issues which may affect the big event. A first step is to confirm whether or not you can even visit the venue beforehand to check the details below. This might prove impossible if you have been asked to present at a distant location, or in the boardroom of another company. If that's the case then you need to be extremely precise in the questions you ask in order to gain the information you require, and double-check these details a few days before you plan to present.

Once the venue has been assessed along the lines suggested below, you may find that it's simply inappropriate for your needs, particularly if you've been asked to present in response to a highly detailed brief with specific demands, such as the delivery of a multi-media display, or which may attract a large audience. By assessing the situation as early as possible, you will be in a position to amend a situation which is working against you and find a good alternative.

So, what do you need to consider?

Room size   Is the room large enough to seat your audience in comfort? Is it, in fact, too big? Cowering in the corner of an echoing chamber will not help establish the aura of intimacy which may be important to the success of your presentation. If this is the case, can it be screened or partitioned, in order to create a more private atmosphere? Movable screens, office dividers, portable display panels, even large floor plants could be used to make a smaller, more appropriate space. If the room is large, will you need amplification if you are to be heard clearly by all members of the audience?

On the other hand, is the room too small? It's a good idea to find a venue with slightly more space than you think you'll need, so that you can accommodate unexpected guests easily without feeling cramped.

Furniture   What furniture is supplied, and who will be arranging it? Don't forget to confirm even the most basic details: enough seats for audience and presenters; suitable furniture to support any audio-visual equipment (see Chapter 5 for more on what you may need); tables for refreshments and handout materials. Think of the needs of your audience as well. If you've planned a presentation which includes written exercises, or one which may demand a lot of note taking, then you'll have to provide desks or tables for your audience as well.

Atmosphere   What is the 'atmosphere' of the room – can it be changed if necessary? If you are using an in-house meeting room, and wish to make a good impression (perhaps on prospective customers) then try to look at your venue through fresh eyes. Is the paintwork scruffy? Could furniture be rearranged to hide dirty skirting boards or marked walls? Is there even time for a quick coat of paint to hide the worst signs of wear and tear? There are a number of instant remedies that can be considered. A simple tablecloth can do wonders for the most basic of tables, and pot plants or fresh flowers can dress a room instantly and to great effect. If the venue is booked in a hotel or conference centre, the manager will be able to help you improve the look of a room if necessary, and you can always pack a tablecloth and bunch of flowers (and vase) in the car to take with you.

Is the furniture mismatched? Try to ensure that the chairs you plan to use are not a raggle-taggle bunch pinched from various offices. If necessary, consider hiring the furniture you require – it's not that expensive for a half or whole day. Is the room too anonymous? Perhaps a wall display is needed to give character and interest to a faceless room, and also to illustrate the main points of your presentation?

Is it appropriate?   Does the venue suit the type of presentation you plan to deliver? If you want to impress a group of clients, should you use the boardroom rather than the oldest meeting room? Is a neutral venue, such as a hotel, better for more contentious presentations?

Power and lighting   How many power points are there and where are they situated? Will you need to pack extension cables in order to use any electrical equipment? Can lighting be changed to suit the type of audio-visual display you have in mind? Does the room have dimmer switches or window blinds?

And what about heating or ventilation? Consider the comfort of your audience – you don't want them to be distracted because they are too cold or too hot.

Entertaining   Is the venue suitable for any entertaining or catering you may have in mind? We'll look at this issue in more detail later in the book, but at this initial stage, make sure that kitchen facilities are available if you need them, or space is available for whatever entertainment you are planning, from a cup of coffee on arrival to a full buffet lunch.

Audio-visual equipment

You've made sure that the venue is suitable for the type of audio-visual display you're planning to use. Now you need to make sure that the equipment you need will be ready for use on the big day.

If you are presenting in a room down the corridor from your office then this task is simpler, but you'll still need to make sure that the equipment is available and working on the day, and can be transported to the room you've reserved without a problem. If you are travelling to present you need to confirm who is providing what, and how it's going to arrive at the venue.

Local trade telephone directories list a wide range of organizations who hire out equipment for individual presentations. Make sure you reserve the equipment you want as early as possible, double-check nearer the time that everything is still according to the master plan, and also build in some time to familiarize yourself with the equipment you are hiring, before you start to present.

Read Chapter 5 when you get to this point in your planning – it gives more information on what you'll need to gather together when using different types of AV equipment.

Planning entertainment or catering

If you are the 'host' of a presentation, then you may want to entertain your audience – perhaps a cup of coffee on arrival, or even a formal dinner after a presentation has been delivered.

If so, confirm the following as quickly as you can:

- The nature and scale of any entertainment.
- The number of people to be entertained (and don't forget to include yourself and your assistants).
- That the venue is appropriate for the type of entertaining you have in mind (see below for more on this important point).
- That caterers are booked well in advance, if needed.

If you plan to offer anything more complicated than tea and coffee, try to use a venue which has two separate 'spaces'. You may not be lucky enough to find two adjoining rooms, but perhaps you can divide the room by means of screens or even just by distance. Arrange the entertainment area by the entrance: coffee or tea can then be set out ready for your guests' arrival and can be replaced by a buffet at the close of the presentation.

Catering must never become intrusive and interrupt the flow of the proceedings: there should be no dirty cups left lying around the venue when you begin to present; the sound of clinking crockery should not interrupt your speech; and the tempting smell of warm food should not start your audience thinking about lunch while you're still trying to make important points. Don't opt for a menu which proves difficult to serve: don't go for a hot buffet if your venue is far from a kitchen; if food is to be laid out in the same room as your presentation choose dishes that can be wheeled in and placed on to the table in a matter of minutes. This can all take place as soon as you have finished speaking (or during the question and answer session) rather than while you are in full flow (even caterers cannot lay out food in the dark, if you're in the middle of a slide show).

Simplicity is the best option, and any efficient caterer will be able to advise on the most appropriate menu for the event you have in mind.

Travel arrangements

Not all presentations take place within easy reach of your office. Once again, now that you've confirmed the venue, run through the following points:

- What time are you expected at the presentation venue?
- Do you know *exactly* where you are going? Do you need a map or transport details?
- Can you get there on time? Do you need to stay near the venue the night before? Do you have to allow for traffic or is public transport a better option? If you have to drive are there any major roadworks or other potential delays which might affect your journey time?
- How will you get your equipment and presentation material there? If you're travelling by train or plane, can you carry all the equipment you need by yourself? Will you need to courier material to your destination, revise your presentation plan, or enlist some additional help?
- How will you get back? Would an overnight stay after the event make life easier, and ensure no one has a long journey home in the dark?
- If you are presenting as a team, do you want to meet up first and then arrive at the venue together?

You want to arrive at your presentation unstressed, fresh and – most importantly – on time. See pages 44–5 for more on what to do if you're running late.

Stage two – planning content

In Chapter 3 we'll look in more detail at how to structure and create the content of your presentation. At this early planning stage, we simply need to identify the tasks this creation phase will entail, who is going to undertake them and how long each task could take.

As you set about the creative process, you'll need to do some or all of the following activities (each of which will be covered in more detail in the next chapter):

■ Brainstorming sessions – to generate initial ideas.

■ Research – if background information is required. This could range from a half day surfing the Internet to a series of in-depth interviews around the country. At this stage try to establish what you need to do, and how much time you can allow yourself to do it.

■ Preparation of drafts and circulation for comment.

■ Obtaining third party approvals – for testimonials, client references or copyright material.

■ Preparation of illustrative materials, and the circulation and checking of drafts.

■ Preparation of handouts, the circulation and checking of drafts and the printing and collating of the final versions.

Let's look at some of these points in more detail:

Writing as a team

Some presentations are group efforts from start to finish, especially those which call upon different experts to provide specific input. In these cases, although the burden of creating the entire presentation does not fall upon one individual, project management needs to be even tighter, as you must clearly identify who is responsible for each section and ensure they meet strict deadlines. Always set your deadlines a little earlier than really necessary – this allows for both the unexpected and for the less reliable individual!

Gaining external approvals

You might need to gain approval from outside sources for some of the material you plan to use – if you want to feature a case history based around the work you have done for another company for example, or mention clients' names as part of a testimonial section. Once again, schedule these milestones well in advance, and keep in mind a contingency plan in case of emergencies. If you need approval from another organization to use their logo or case history, for example, why not negotiate unlimited approval for all future presentations – this will help save time in the future. Further information on copyright is covered in the following chapter.

Preparing back-up presentations

If you are planning a particularly sophisticated, multi-media display, make sure that if the worst comes to the worst and your equipment fails, the main points of your talk can be made using handheld notes and OHP transparencies and/or hard copies of your visuals. As we will see later in this chapter, even the best laid plans can go wrong, especially when presenting in a venue you have never visited. The more complex the presentation, and the more it relies upon factors beyond your control (modem links, complex software, even a simple electrical supply) the greater the chances of something happening to undermine your plans. An 'insurance policy' back-up presentation will give you peace of mind, especially when delivering a more complicated presentation. You may also be able to use it in rehearsals, and recycle it if you need to give the presentation again in less formal circumstances.

Reviewing drafts

It's important to build in several review periods when putting your presentation together, and to try to enlist the help of someone outside your immediate band of helpers. Ask him or her to look over your presentation notes, your visuals and your handouts, as and when they are prepared. Then ask him or her to review your material twice: once for content, style and consistency; secondly for grammar and spelling. This latter point is most important when reviewing visual or printed material (as we all know that even spell checkers are not infallible). For some unknown reason, it is often the sentence in the largest typeface that contains a dreadful misspelling, or which misses out certain words altogether – and no one notices until it's up on the screen. Don't ask anyone who has read your material two or three times, or who is familiar with the content, to proof-read your work. It needs a fresh eye to point out the obvious mistakes.

In Chapter 5, we look at some basic points of grammar which can help you avoid potentially embarrassing *faux pas*.

Preparing illustrations

If you plan to present using visual aids then the brief for the text, graphics and design will fall out of the first draft of the presentation script. You'll also find that you can probably include visuals from other presentations as well. Writing text for visuals is covered in Chapter 5 but at this early planning stage you need to decide:

■ who will be preparing illustrative material: yourself, your colleagues or an external agency? Whoever has the responsibility, make sure he or she has this commitment firmly booked into his or her diary.

■ whether copyright or other approvals will be required. It might be useful to start to build up a library of pre-approved or 'copyright free' material which can be drawn upon at short notice, to avoid delays in the future.

Planning handout material

It's a sad fact of business life, but you have to accept that your audience will remember little of what you say unless they have taken notes or notes are provided: and so most audiences expect handouts to accompany even the most informal presentation. Handout material acts as the tangible reminder of who you were and what you had to say. It's also a way of providing further information on key points, supplying relevant background information, and details on the presenter or team and the organization they represent.

What to prepare?

Obviously, the material you put together in support of your presentation depends entirely on the content you deliver and the nature of the audience, but in general, your handouts should represent a mix of core and supportive material:

Core material

■ A timetable of the presentation
■ Copies of visual aids
■ Notes for exercises or workshops
■ Lists of key points
■ Feedback forms (see Chapter 7 for more information)
■ 'Potted biographies' of the presenter or team and contact details
■ A proposal document, if needed.

Supportive material

■ Brochures, leaflets or other material on the organization or individual presenting, and on the subject being presented

■ Contextual material, supporting the presentation. This can include: photocopies of press cuttings, articles, case studies in relevant areas

■ Additional references or sources of further information.

Double-check the expected audience numbers nearer the time to make sure you have prepared enough sets of handouts – and make sure you have some to spare.

In certain scenarios, such as a competitive pitch, the presentation may be supported by a longer document – a proposal – which lays out in more detail the points being made: The Marvellous Marketing team will be preparing such a proposal document. This book does not cover the production of such complex documents, but it's important to note that the work required to produce them can impact heavily upon presentation planning and can greatly affect the resources you have available to prepare the presentation. Planning needs to be even more controlled if proposal documents are to be produced, and a second project manager may even be needed to make sure it is delivered on time.

Handout material should retain as professional an appearance as possible. This will add weight and importance to your presentation, and also imply your respect of your audience. If a number of different pieces of information are to be given out, consider investing in some sort of folder to hold them all together. If you are presenting to colleagues, then this need not be too elaborate. A variety of relatively inexpensive wallets and folders exist which can be customized – by the use of DTP and word processing – into smart document folders for presentation information. If your organization presents regularly to external audiences then it's probably worth investing in a document wallet overprinted with your company name, and with enough room inside to carry a number of different items. Such wallets can also include small slots allowing the insertion of a business card. And don't simply print everything out in black and white: colour laser printers are now easily available and although the cartridges are expensive and output can be slow, they produce attractive and engaging documents that will continue to work for you after you have left the stage.

Follow on material

Always invite your audience to ask for additional sets of handouts, or other information, and offer to send it on to them if necessary. In certain circumstances, you could also offer to send on a full transcript of the presentation just delivered – if it's a press launch, for example, or your presentation included a guest speaker making an interesting speech. If you plan to offer this service, then make sure you either have a transcript already drafted (which you can change at the last minute if necessary), or alternatively, record the event on tape and prepare a transcript afterwards.

Rehearsals and practice

Rehearsals should be timetabled into your planning schedule right from the start. Although there is a limit to how early you can start to rehearse, it may be useful for both you and your presentation team to book in more specific 'practice' time earlier on if necessary – perhaps to brush up on a particular skill, or to become more familiar with a piece of presentation equipment.

Full rehearsals need to imitate the final presentation as closely as possible: you must use the same notes, the same equipment and so on. Book your rehearsals early on in the planning process to ensure you have a suitable room and the appropriate equipment available when you need it. Rehearsals will highlight those areas which may have been neglected or simply overlooked so it's wise not to schedule such a rehearsal too close to the real event or you may find you have to rewrite parts of your core presentation speech with little or no time to rehearse the changes.

Even if you are giving a presentation which has been honed to perfection, a dress rehearsal will still be valuable – perhaps not every time the presentation is needed, but certainly every now and again. New ideas may occur to you as you practise tested material; certain elements may need to be updated; and it is always wise to guard against complacency and ensure the presentation sounds as fresh as if you were delivering it for the very first time.

No matter how informal the presentation, a rehearsal will do wonders for the end result. Very few presentations are given entirely off the cuff – and if they are, it is because the material has been presented many times before and therefore practised time and time again.

When you rehearse, keep the following points in mind:

■ Does the presentation last for the correct time?
■ Is the start of the presentation suitably arresting?

- Do the points flow in a logical manner?
- Are introductions and hand-overs handled smoothly?
- Is everyone comfortable with the equipment being used?
- How are questions handled?
- Does the whole thing 'gel'?

As we work through this book, we'll cover each of these areas in more depth, enabling you to assess the results of your rehearsals effectively.

Team presentations will probably need more rehearsal time, and this should be taken into account when scheduling. You'll want to focus on particular aspects of the presentation – handovers, style, handling questions and answers – in the context of team dynamics.

Rehearsing question and answer sessions is also very important. As we will see later on, predicting the questions you may be asked and preparing your answers in advance is part of the presentation planning procedure. But you still must be prepared to handle the real event, with no conferring! The best method is to rehearse in front of an audience of colleagues, including a few who are not involved in the planning process. Give them the brief so that they are aware of the overall aims of the presentation. The questions they throw you at the end of the rehearsal will test your ability to think on the spot and also put your prepared answers under the spotlight.

If your presentation is absolutely crucial to the success of the company, or if you or your team has a history of failure when presenting, then consider calling in a professional to view your rehearsals – perhaps someone who trains presenters for a living. Although this will be an expensive exercise, the results – especially if they actually win you business – may be worth it.

Professional training

From time to time, we all need to brush up our business skills , and presentations are no exception, especially if one doesn't present regularly.

As your presentation comes ever closer, you may decide that now is the time to book some training sessions. Professional training can be particularly useful, especially if you need to:

- practise skills
- check the development of bad habits
- learn about, use and assess the latest equipment

■ practice in a focused but less stressful environment.

Training can be implemented in two main ways: by attending a training course or by organizing an in-house, tailor-made training session. The option you choose depends greatly on the nature of your business and how often you present.

Independently organized training courses offer a number of advantages. Employees can be sent on the course one by one, as they join the company, or as they need to gather presentation skills, and such courses bring together people from different organizations who can pool experience. If you work in a business which uses the presentation as one of its main communication tools then it is probably best to find a training course held specifically for people working in your industry – it will focus more closely on your business needs, and the other delegates will bring relevant experience to the course. Trade bodies and professional organizations often provide such courses.

The other alternative is the tailor-made course, delivered in-house. This can prove more expensive but if you have a large enough group it could be more cost-effective than sending them all away. Fees, travel, accommodation (if necessary) and other expenses can soon mount up.

When commissioning an in-house course, make sure you think about exactly what you need, and brief the training organization carefully. As a first step, clarify the following points:

■ What are your organization's needs, especially within the context of the industry in which you operate? What types of presentation do you give, how often, who to, and why? What are the features of your industry that a trainer would need to know about. (For example, do your staff mainly travel to present? Do they usually present as a team? Do you present as a marketing activity or as a way of communicating information?)

■ How many staff need presentation training? Are they all at the same level of experience, or are different levels of training required?

■ Do you need training on specific presentation technologies? Or would you like to have a session looking at all the possible options?

A tailored course can either be held on your premises or 'off-site', which can have its advantages (although obviously the cost of room hire and refreshments will add to the final bill). The opportunity to concentrate on the matter in hand away from the everyday distractions of the office can help delegates gain even more from the training provided.

Establish a budget

The allocation of a budget for each presentation should become an automatic part of the planning procedure – but it's often forgotten in the enthusiasm to do the best you or your team possibly can. The costs associated with preparing a presentation are important and can mount up alarmingly, and so they must be estimated and balanced against the outcome at this early stage.

Any or all of the following may form a part of a presentation – and could add up to quite a lot if not controlled:

- Room hire
- Hire or purchase of AV equipment
- Training
- Photography, design and the production of illustrations and handouts
- Research fees
- Accommodation
- Travel
- Entertainment

And don't forget the 'cost' of your colleagues' time – if they are important income earners for your organization, then the time they spend on your presentation must be worth the final, desirable outcome.

Allocate a sum for each different item early on in the planning process, as it will be one of the factors guiding your decision making.

Drafting a schedule

You've identified the various elements that will go to make your presentation a success, and you know how long you've got to pull it all together. The next step is to draw up a plan that will physically lay out these elements within a defined framework.

Such a plan can be created in a variety of ways. An office wallplanner can provide a useful format or, alternatively, create a dedicated chart that will give you 'time lines' linking each task to its deadline and highlighting the individual stages that fall in between. The team at Marvellous Marketing have put together such a plan – after all, theirs is a complex presentation on which much depends, so concrete planning is essential. Let's see the end result – remember their brief has already been confirmed, so they can concentrate purely on delivery:

WEEK ONE	
Fri:	— Meeting with client/visit venue (am)
	— Brainstorming session/identify research needs/ delegate responsibilities
	— Set budget/contact designer (pm)
	— Start proposal – Fergus to manage
WEEK TWO	
Mon:	/
Tue:	/
Wed:	— Progress meeting/review 1st draft proposal and presentation script: circulate for comments
	— Start first draft visuals
Thur:	— Comments returned – incorporate, plus research results; start on handouts
Fri:	— Brief designer on OHPs
WEEK THREE	
Mon:	— Progress meeting
Tue:	— Circulate 2nd draft
Wed:	— First rehearsal/review handouts
Thur:	— View OHP designs – revise if necessary/2nd draft returned
Fri:	— Second rehearsal

WEEK FOUR
Mon: Progress meeting/review comments on 2nd draft
Tue: Revised OHPs returned
Wed: Third rehearsal/circulate 3rd draft
Thur: Fourth rehearsal if necessary/confirm 3rd as final draft
Fri: Print/collate handouts

WEEK FIVE
Mon: Final double-checking/final meeting
Tue: PRESENT!

And what about Tom Collins? He has more time to play with, but administratively a potentially more complex presentation. Tom chooses a straightforward list of key deadlines to mark the major steps in his planning:

SEPTEMBER – ASAP
— Full briefing meeting with Helen J
— Visit venue/confirm technical facilities and requirements
— Provide synopsis for advance publicity

OCTOBER
— Confirm equipment needed – hire/borrow?
— Revise brochure/arrange for reprint

NOV/DEC
— Draft presentation/rehearse – think about visuals and handouts. Draft timetable
— Shortlist potential Web Sites to visit in presentation
— Book van to transport equipment?
— Confirm numbers expected
— Rehearse outline

DON'T FORGET THE XMAS HOLIDAYS!!!

JAN
— Final confirmation of details
— 2 x technical rehearsal in office
— Double-check Web Sites – download examples onto disk just
  in case
— Finalize presentation and visuals
— Prepare OHP back-up presentation
— Prepare handouts
— Full rehearsal in venue if possible

And Sarah Williams? Well, she needs your help, so you'll find more on her plans at the end of this chapter.

Planning to meet the impossible deadline!

The ultimate nightmare – you're asked to give an important presentation with hardly any warning. Given the wealth of instructions above, how could you possibly hope to cover the same ground in what could be as little as a few hours? Take heed of the following advice:

■ First and most important, don't panic. Don't flap around your office grabbing at anything and everything, and making desperate telephone calls to enlist assistance that you don't know what to do with.

■ Just as before, list – as quickly as you can – the essence of the brief: Where and when are you going to present? Who will be in the audience and what do they want to hear? How are you going to tell them? Create an immediate deadline plan and stick to it!

■ Don't concentrate on what you haven't got but on what you have. Any organization which presents even semi-regularly will have generated an archive of material which can be plundered. If it's stored on PC, even better – it can be updated or edited immediately to meet the new brief. Don't forget colleagues in other departments who present, even if they talk on completely different subjects. Do they have cartoons or stock graphics you could borrow to add instant colour or humour to your presentation? Raiding the archives should provide a good beginning – your recycled visuals might not match the brief exactly, but your script may be able to overcome this with a little fine tuning.

- If you want to use visual aids, choose a technique which will deliver the most professional result with the minimum of preparation time – Chapter 5 goes through all the possibilities.

- Identify where the gaps are in your material, and try to condense them as much as possible, so that you have a minimum of new material to prepare and to put onto accompanying visual aids.

- Don't be over-ambitious – it's better to do a simple presentation well than to deliver an over-complicated, poorly thought out presentation due to lack of time (over which you had no control).

- Handouts are difficult to put together at short notice – focus on producing copies of your visuals or simply compile a selection of brochures, datasheets or other relevant, available information and place into a wallet or folder. You can always promise to send on further information after the presentation, when you have more time to present it properly.

- Learn from this experience and be prepared. File all completed presentation materials carefully – presentation scripts and notes, visuals, and a full set of handouts – and keep the same records on disk for immediate retrieval. Many people who present regularly also keep a skeleton presentation ready and waiting, and amass information which can be slotted in as appropriate. This is especially true of any organization which often wins business by presenting. If a professional, polished and appropriate presentation can be delivered at very short notice, then it can make a particularly good impression.

- One word of warning about standard presentations. Review regularly and carefully: it's amazing how quickly even the most mundane piece of information can go out of date, and how easy it is to forget about new, more powerful material.

Contingency planning – expecting the unexpected

A presentation can hold a multitude of surprises, especially if it takes place in a room you have never used before. The venue is often the cause of many unpleasant surprises, but that's not the only way things can go wrong. What should you dread and how can you prepare for it?

The venue changes at the last minute

Don't waste time ranting and raving (save that for later on). Check the vital statistics of the new venue against your action plan checklist, and aim to answer the most essential questions:

- Do you have to change travel plans or arrangements for entertaining?
- Do you have to change your presentation techniques?

If the new venue renders your presentation concept unusable, you may have some fast thinking to do. If the change was simply unavoidable (a leaking roof, for example, or a double-booking that was not your fault), your audience should accept any shortcomings in your delivery and will be generally sympathetic. Remember, if you have your emergency presentation to hand, then you should be able to present, whatever the circumstances.

Your audio-visual equipment fails

The more technically complex the presentation, I'm afraid, the more likely this is to happen. Once again, the golden rule applies: a back-up presentation will never let you down, so make sure you prepare it just as carefully as the one you would ideally like to deliver.

You're running late

The ultimate nightmare: your presentation is ready, your visuals sharp, your handouts immaculate, and you're stuck in a major traffic jam with no sign of movement.

Lateness is often due to disorganization. Last-minute rushing around to complete tasks that should have been done earlier will leave you with no margin of error when you set off on your journey. Rushing causes you to make mistakes, and means you'll arrive at your presentation flustered and worried about those all-important details (and probably late), even if you're only going to an in-house meeting room. So if you've followed all the advice given so far in this book, that eventuality won't happen!

However, we all know that if you travel, the result can be anything but predictable – and so communication becomes increasingly important if you find yourself unexpectedly delayed.

The ubiquitous mobile phone is a godsend in such situations, so if you have to travel to present, make sure your phone is fully charged and with you all the time. If you think you'll be late, try to assess this as early as you possibly can, and phone ahead with the news. Suggest that the presentation is delayed by an appropriate time, or if you are part of a wider programme, suggest that the running order is changed to accommodate your unexpected delay. Make sure you still give yourself enough time to arrive, freshen up and go through your preparations as necessary. You don't want to say you'll be 15 minutes late, which turns out to be 30, and causes you to rush, panicking into the venue; or to be ringing your contact every 20 minutes revising your estimated arrival time.

Major hold-ups do occur, and even the best laid plans go wrong, so if your reason is genuine then your host or audience should be realistic and forgiving. If the worst comes to the worst, ask if you can rearrange the presentation for much later that same day, or even on another day if it means that key members of your audience can still attend. However, if you do have to travel along a route notorious for hold-ups (and we can probably all think of many major highways that fit this bill) allow yourself enough extra time to avoid the everyday jams and slow-moving traffic, as your audience won't be so impressed if you simply underestimated the journey time.

The venue proves difficult to find

If you are hosting the event at a neutral venue, take some simple signs along with you to use in the lobby or entrance to the building to ensure a minimum of delay when your audience arrives. Add a sign to the door of the room you are using to help latecomers enter with confidence. Many conference venues can provide such signage for you.

Your presentation could suffer from interruptions

Nothing is more intrusive than an unexpected head appearing around the door checking to see if the room is being used, which is most likely to happen if you are using a common meeting room in your own building, or a room in a venue such as a hotel or institution. If you think that this is likely to happen, take along a small sign saying 'meeting in progress' which can be fixed to the door during your presentation.

The furniture is of the right type but the wrong sort

Of course, your advance planning and liaison will have made sure that the venue suits the presentation you plan to deliver, but – and especially when dealing with third parties – you may have thought you were talking about the same thing when, upon arrival it's clear that you weren't. A table, for example, can mean very different things to different people. The table isn't big enough for the OHP and your notes; it's too low to use as a lectern, as you had planned; the table provided is a boardroom table around which everyone is expected to sit, making your OHP very awkward to use . . . the permutations are endless.

The only way to avoid an unpleasant surprise is to visit the venue ahead of time – even if it's only ten minutes before you start presenting. This will give you enough time to rearrange the available furniture or even find alternatives if it doesn't fit the bill. If your presentation relies heavily upon your AV equipment, and you are travelling to the venue by car, it might even be worth taking a collapsible table with you to make sure you have exactly what you need.

The presentation is a more formal occasion than you expected

The only way to avoid potential embarrassment is always to assume a greater formality than otherwise supposed. You don't want to be told, at the last minute, that the chairman of the board will be 'sitting in' on your presentation, when you've decided to wear jeans and a T-shirt. We'll look at strategies for personal presentation in a later chapter, but in general, it's much easier to turn a formal suit into a more relaxed outfit by simply removing a jacket than trying to dress up casual clothes. Alternatively, if your workplace is already fairly informal, bring a jacket with you on the big day, to provide an optional quick change.

Your audience is larger than you expected

If space allows, always arrange for a few extra chairs to be left in the room you are using. Additional guests can then be accommodated without wasting time looking for additional seating and bringing it back to the venue.

It's also wise to prepare more sets of handout material than you expect to use, as you can never predict who will turn up, or who would like to take a set of notes back to their colleagues. Another good idea is to take a hard bound 'visitors book' with you: if your audience exceeds your estimate, then ask delegates to write their details in the book, which can be left at the entrance to the room, and then post on sets of handouts as soon as you get back to your office.

You or a member of your team are ill

But you remembered to make sure you had an understudy didn't you? (See page 27.) Well, as we all know, life is not always that straightforward, but if it's a vital presentation then it is wise to make sure someone is available to stand in if necessary. If you hadn't earmarked someone for such a role, then ask one of those who helped you prepare, or watched you rehearse. He or she will at least be familiar with the concept and the running order of the presentation. As we mentioned earlier, if you have to call upon a colleague at the last minute, try to choose someone with many presentations already under their belt. His or her confidence will help overcome nerves, and also help manage and cover the mistakes which will undoubtedly happen.

As a matter of courtesy, inform both the organizers of your presentation and your audience as soon as you can that the presenter has changed: if you can do this before everyone has gathered in the venue, you may find that they are willing to wait until the presenter has recovered, and so the event can be postponed.

Summary

■ Appoint a project manager capable of overseeing all planning procedures and managing a team whilst still being able to pay attention to fine detail.

■ Prepare a planning timetable: identify all the tasks you need to complete, estimate how long they'll take and clarify all deadlines.

- Make sure all personnel involved are informed well in advance, including any stand-ins you might need.
- Assess the suitability of the venue as early as possible and identify your audio visual needs, catering and travel arrangements.
- Outline the tasks you need to complete to create the content of your presentation.
- Book rehearsals well in advance, and any equipment you might need to rehearse with: book training as early as possible.
- Don't forget to establish a budget.
- A cool head and continuous, ongoing preparation will help you meet the most impossible deadline.
- Prepare for the unexpected!

Do it yourself

We've seen Marvellous Marketing drawing up their planning schedule, and also looked at Tom Collins' notes. What about our third example?

Sarah Williams has been asked to oversee the planning of the presentation to new recruits and needs a schedule fast – she only has a week in which to get organized, even though the presentation is relatively simple. What should she do? Using the format of a straightforward list, note down her key actions and deadlines.

3 | CREATING A SUCCESSFUL PRESENTATION

Everything is now underway. The brief has been agreed, goals are clearly defined and organization is under control. Now all you have to do is write the presentation!

So where to start?

Your subject matter should be reasonably clear cut, especially if the brief has been well defined. The challenge is to design, create and deliver a presentation that responds to the brief by covering all the most relevant points in an arresting, compelling manner which will engage the audience and achieve your original aims. Simple!

Let's divide this process into a number of stages:

- List all the points that have to be made.
- Order the points that have to be made.
- Think, creatively, about *how* to make each point.
- Confirm any research that has to be done to help you support each point.

Now let's look at each of these stages in more detail:

List the points that must be made

If you are to present a straightforward topic which you know inside out, then listing your main points should be easy – but not if you have to talk about a subject which needs research, or which touches on a range of different issues, or is being delivered in response to a specific challenge (take our Marvellous Marketing team for example, now researching the intricacies of exporting industrial instruments).

Whatever the scenario, a good way to begin is to get down on paper – in no particular order – all the points you can think of. A brainstorming session is a good way to get started.

Brainstorming

If your presentation covers a lot of ground, or would benefit from new ideas and a little creativity, then it's a good idea to enlist the help of others in a brainstorming session. Invite along all those who are closely involved with the presentation and include a few who know nothing about the subject matter. They might have valuable comments to make, and may reflect more accurately the viewpoint of the audience.

Some people say that a true brainstorm should last no more than 15 minutes, during which time everyone should shout out ideas as they come to them, fast and furiously. But as a presentation brief is usually quite circumscribed, a less 'chaotic' approach may prove more fruitful, as it allows people to think more constructively about the subject matter in hand.

The best way to manage a presentation brainstorm is to assemble all your participants in a room, go over the brief you have been given (to ensure everyone has the same information) and then open the floor to suggestions. Appoint one person to act as facilitator – to manage the discussion, provoke new directions and to make sure all voices are heard. Designate someone to write down each point as it is made: this could be done on a flip chart or black/white board, or even better, on self-stick notes which are then stuck to the wall. Order is not important at this point, and try to prevent the participants getting involved in discussions of the merit of individual points. That comes at the next stage.

J. Jonathan Gabay in *Teach Yourself Copywriting* (Hodder and Stoughton, 1996), lists the following 'nine rules of effective brainstorming' which provide useful guidelines for facilitators:

1 Every brainstormer is equal.
2 No brainstormer is permitted to evaluate another brainstormer's ideas.
3 The more off-the-wall an idea the better [although this may not be quite so practical in a presentation context].
4 All ideas can be coupled and encouraged.
5 Never mind about the quality, feel the width. Brainstorm sessions should generate long lists of ideas, however good or bad those ideas may be.
6 Include every idea in the final list. To censor ideas is to judge them.

7 Brainstormers cannot ask leading or intimidating questions. For example 'Don't you agree that when it comes to experience of this kind of thing, my idea must surely be the best?'

8 Whether an idea sounds good or odd, let curiosity encourage it to be developed.

9 Once you have all agreed on the most accurate and informed creative options, let the final analysis take pure 'gut feeling' or intuition into account.

A brainstorming session may seem a little grand for the presentation you are planning but you will find that two or more heads are better than one, and you may be surprised by the unexpected avenues of thought a little collaboration will encourage. Your co-brainstormers' responses will also be invaluable in confirming that you are on the right track, and also to highlight any omissions that you might have made or to suggest additional material that you could include.

Confirm the order of points to be made

Remember the three point rule: tell them what you're going to say; say it; then tell them what you've just said. That, in essence, is the order of your presentation. Sounds easy enough, but when you've got a lot of information to put across, including points of equal value, the whole process can become more complex. Once you've established your list of points, keep the following hints in mind, and this stage should become easier:

Look for a logical flow through

Look for links between your points that will enable your presentation to flow and therefore sound more coherent. If you have to make a number of equally important but perhaps less closely related points, are there any subgroups into which you could divide your information? Group your points accordingly and look for balance – if a certain issue covers a lot of ground, perhaps it should go at the front, or divided into smaller groups of points which can be independently framed. Are you building up to a main argument or single revelation? You may want to aim for a crescendo effect, building up to your most important point by a careful stepping stone arrangement of other information.

Make the most of your good points

If you are selling yourself then you must make sure your audience remembers key information about you. Undergo a brief analysis of your strengths and weaknesses in the context of the brief, and let this influence the way you order your points. If possible, repeat these good points at regular intervals as you proceed.

Create dramatic impact

If your presentation is to pack a few surprises, then decide immediately where they're going to be – at the start, as a striking beginning, or leading up to a grand finale? By placing your most important point in the order first, you can gain the attention of your audience – as long as the remainder of your presentation doesn't feel like an anti-climax.

Remember your hidden agenda

Look back to your earlier analysis – do any hidden agendas influence the way you need to order your points? Will certain sections of the audience be more interested in some issues than others, whatever their overall importance? Do you have a specific argument that needs to be promoted, within a broader context? It may be that 'office politics' will dictate the order in which certain items are introduced. You can exploit the audience's interest by saving what is perhaps the most interesting part (from their point of view) until last. As a result they pay more attention to the rest of the presentation, rather than losing interest quickly.

Creative thinking

You may think that there is no room for creativity in the presentation you have to deliver: perhaps you have to explain pension rights to a group of new employees, or explain the intricacies of the archiving system to your organization's administrative assistants. But it is precisely the dullest, most limited subject matter which is in greatest need of the most creativity, that extra sparkle which makes a presentation memorable. It's also often the case that the most 'boring' subject matter is the one of most importance to the individuals present, so a high level of understanding and recall may be one of your key goals, whatever the nature of the material you plan to deliver.

When should you take a creative approach? Well, you don't need to turn creative cartwheels in order to explain every point, but perhaps it could be applied to visual aids? To the examples you use? To the introduction or to the conclusion, even to the accompanying handout material? Perhaps you need to organize a second brainstorming meeting to get your mind working on *how* to present the points you need to make.

A number of techniques exist which can be used to stimulate new ideas, and new approaches to a subject. Whether used in a group brainstorm session or by an individual, creative thinking techniques aim to disrupt the normal thought patterns that most of us employ – the well-worn trains of thought into which we all fall. How to get yourself off those tramlines and into unexplored mental territory? Here are two techniques that might be worth considering, and you will find many more in books which focus more closely on the subject:

Mind mapping

Take a piece of paper, flip chart or wall board, and write your core topic in the centre. Then, using this central word as a starting point, start to make lists of all the words that come into your mind. For example:

Sales targets – target practice – bow and arrow – Robin Hood – Sherwood Forest – forest walks – holidays – money

From that string you might be able to develop at least one unusual illustration – Robin Hood – to support what might be a rather heavy topic, plus one linking idea – increased sales means better holidays – which can provide a good verbal illustration of the point you wish to make.

Let's look at a more extensive mind map for the topic puzzling our Marvellous Marketing team. They've placed the word 'export' at the centre of their map, and are feeling a little challenged. After a few minutes' effort, what have they come up with? Figure 3.1 is the result.

And what could they get out of it? Well, for a start, they know they will have to do some research on world currencies and financial situations, such as the Euro and the EMU and make sure their knowledge of related issues is up to the minute. Perhaps they could use some of the images they have come up with as backdrops for their visuals – stereotypes, they know, but images of paperwork or container ships might just lift their presentation. And what about the Award idea – could they do some

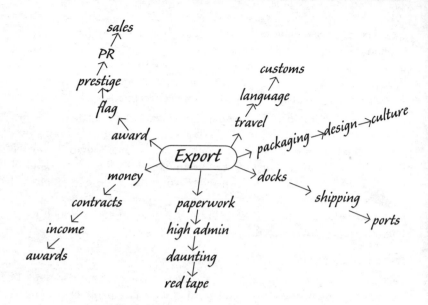

Figure 3.1   Marvellous Marketing's mind map

research on what business awards could be entered for, perhaps building on the flag idea, for example shipping/flags/corporate honour?

Once again, at this stage the results are pretty haphazard, but the creative juices have started, and more ideas will flow as they start to warm to their theme.

Dropped dictionary

This seemingly impossible method can stimulate some quite surprising results. Take a dictionary and literally drop it on the floor, letting it fall open quite randomly. Then, close your eyes and place a finger on the page in order to choose a word. This word then forms your starting point (you may have to try a couple of times to settle on a word which isn't too outrageous, but don't keep going until you've found a word that seems to suit your needs – that is the opposite of what you are trying to achieve). Keeping your subject matter in mind, list all the ideas, associations, images or whatever that come to you when you think of the word that the dictionary has selected.

Here's an example: our hapless presenter faced with the topic of 'pension rights' drops his dictionary in despair. The word randomly selected is 'Jonah'. What could we get out of that?

> whales – eating – swallowing – fish in the sea – Moby Dick – bad luck – bible – lost at sea – jinx – Pinnochio – fairy story – cartoon – song – puppet – wood –

. . . and so the list goes on.

How could this be used to enliven a worthy but dull subject? Perhaps some allegories could be developed: Do most people consider pension companies or funds to be huge whales, swallowing up their small investments and then coughing them up when the time comes? Are pensions a frightening thought? Do most people feel like puppets at the hands of those who handle the money? Perhaps some humorous illustrations could be developed to lead into each section of the presentation?

Well, it obviously needs more thought, but already our presenter is feeling a little more excited at the prospect of delivering the presentation, because it is already sounding and looking vibrant and alive, and will be far more interesting to plan and deliver.

Adding emphasis – supportive material

Expanding and illustrating core information with unusual facts, research findings or background detail can result in a much more engaging and interesting presentation, and can also demonstrate your enthusiasm to do well (if that is one of your goals) by the effort you have put into researching the topic in hand. What information could you use?

Consider:

- Survey results, proven statistics, 'official figures' that can be attributed to a reliable source.
- Headlines from relevant news media, or quotes from respected journalists.
- 'Famous quotations' from any individual relevant to the subject matter or audience.
- Comments from those people in whom the audience is most interested (for example, its customers; its competitors; its shareholders).
- Cartoons or other relevant illustrations.

Supportive material can be used in a variety of ways:

- ■ To back up arguments or hypotheses.
- ■ To push home points that need additional emphasis.
- ■ To add humour and lighten a mood.
- ■ To inject colour and variety.

Sources of information

Survey results? Competitor comments? Surely this will all take too long to generate? Not so: in this age of modern technology a lot more information is at your fingertips than you may realize. Here are a few places to start looking.

The Internet

Anyone familiar with the Internet will know that it is an unrivalled source of information on almost any topic you can think of, although the quality of the information found can vary quite considerably. The Internet also allows you to research at any time of day or night, and to keep a log of what you've found.

When planning a presentation, look out for the following types of Web Site as useful sources of information (and many of these will provide links to other associated sites):

- ■ Government departments – these can provide statistical information, press releases, official quotes, summaries of reports and so on.
- ■ Well-known information providers such as trade bodies, voluntary societies, and charities. Many home pages provide links to other related sites which can expand your search into unexpectedly fruitful areas.
- ■ Major commercial organizations: many carry useful information which extends beyond corporate facts and figures (although these can also prove very useful).

When using the Internet, make sure you understand and can use all the search facilities on offer – not only will you save valuable time, but you will find far more relevant Sites. Once at a chosen Web Site, make sure the host seems to be a reliable source, and check when the information was last updated to give you an idea of how accurate it will be. Make sure you don't infringe copyright when using any of the information you've found (see pages 60–2 for more details).

On-line information services

As indicated, although the Internet can provide a seemingly limitless amount of information, quality control is not its forte, and there are also many subjects which will not produce any valuable search results.

Commercially produced, subscription only, on-line information services are becoming increasingly popular among companies who rely upon a constant flow of reliable, regularly updated information – more than they can get merely by accessing the Internet. Such services are not cheap but they offer access to much better quality information, and can be searched with a greater degree of sophistication. If you only need to use such a resource occasionally, try to find an organization that can undertake a search for you for a small fee.

Libraries

With the recent growth in information technology, libraries are promoting themselves much more as active information providers rather than repositories of knowledge, and even the most modest local branch library can offer electronic access to much wider resources. However, if you are planning to use a library for research, then a copyright, university or major public library would be the best place to go. University or research libraries often offer business membership for a fee, which allows access to a wide range of resources, including CD-ROM databases and media archives which can prove to be fruitful hunting grounds for statistics, quotes and other information.

The Media

Newspapers, magazines, periodicals: a good source of all manner of supportive material including statistics, surveys, illustrations and cartoons, quotes from relevant individuals and so on. But how can you track down relevant information from volumes of back copies? Look out for the following resources:

- Many 'quality' newspapers now publish regular archives (mainly of feature articles and main news reports) on CD-ROM or via the Internet, and these can be searched on key words. Accessing this information via the Internet is not free (although some newspapers publish a daily Internet summary free of charge). If you don't subscribe, then you will have to find an organization which does, for example a research library or business information resource, or a friendly company who may be able to let you use their resources for an appropriate fee.

■ Some business magazines are also published in electronic format, but once again, these resources will be found at major libraries or on the Internet, available on subscription.

■ Back copies of an important trade magazine can sometimes be obtained from the publisher, and annual indexes are sometimes produced to accompany journals.

■ TV and radio broadcasts can also contain interesting information, perhaps that could be used as visually illustrative rather than supportive material. Unless you know that a programme is coming on, and can tape it, obtaining a copy is not as easy as looking through back copies of a newspaper. Agencies do exist which tape every programme that's broadcast, and then sell the tapes on, mainly to PR agencies or to organizations who have been featured on air. National broadcasters can sometimes provide transcripts of TV or radio programmes as well, if requested.

Once again, when using such material, remember the copyright laws – see pages 60–2 for more detail.

'Qualitative' market research

If statistics simply don't exist to prove a particular point, then why not generate your own, using 'qualitative' market research? It need not take long and the results, although obviously limited in scope, can still have considerable impact and will certainly impress your audience.

Qualitative market research is a pragmatic alternative to quantitative research. Quantitative research generates information by asking questions of large numbers of relevant individuals, and results are based on the statistical analysis of large numbers of responses. Qualitative research places its emphasis not on the *numbers* of individuals asked, but on the *type*, and the individuals questioned are chosen because they are representative of a large number of like-minded others. Such suitably influential individuals could include:

- editors or journalists within relevant media
- representatives of professional organizations such as trade bodies, voluntary organizations, government-sponsored initiatives and so on
- independent experts in a particular field, such as management consultants, or business analysts, university researchers
- relevant individuals within large, influential companies or other commercial organizations.

The easiest way to undertake a qualitative survey is by phone. Draft a script of exactly what you want to say and test it both on a colleague and a friendly outsider, and test it again on the phone to ensure it really works. When drafting the questionnaire, focus on two or three questions which can be answered in a matter of minutes. If you're talking to people from a range of different categories, you'll find you have to tweak your questionnaire to fit each group – business people won't share the same concerns or have the same viewpoint as journalists for example. Contact details can be obtained from the Internet, from magazines or from the trade telephone directory.

You may find that such a brief survey acts as a prompt for broader discussion but if not, don't push it. Telephone surveys are always an irrelevant interruption to a working day – but as most of us know that our own organization is probably using the same technique, most of us are happy enough to answer a few questions as long as they are short and to the point.

The comments questionnaires generate can either be used statistically (for example, '85 per cent of respondents felt they weren't using the Internet as effectively as they could be'), or anecdotally ('I know the Internet will prove important for my business in the future, but I don't know where to start to make the most of it'). Keep quotes anonymous, unless permission has been sought.

In-house archive

If you work in an organization which regularly presents, then it's worth building up an in-house archive of useful information which can be drawn upon in a hurry. Start to collect (and put into some form of reasonable order) the items in the following list. You may find you already have plenty of such material simply lying around the office:

- Copies of major feature articles from useful publications, including cuttings from the daily quality press.
- A note of good Web Sites.
- Relevant reports or other information: circulars from industry bodies; Government information and so on.
- 'Case history' information, to illustrate specific points. If not already approved for external use, check that permission is given for its use in a presentation.

Copyright

Copyright is a thorny – and potentially litigious – issue, and it's important to get it right. If in doubt, ask one of the official bodies set up to help you (contact details are given at the back of this book).

Please note that the following information refers to UK copyright law. For international variations, contact your own national advisory body.

If you are presenting copyright material for the purposes of criticism or review of that or other material or using it for private purposes, then copyright need not be formally obtained for any material used, as long as credit is given. This will take the form of written acknowledgement to the publication and author, placed alongside any material you have used (whether verbatim or inprecis, in hand-outs or overhead projection or transparencies), and likewise for photos, cartoons or illustrations. You can establish who owns the original copyright by contacting the publisher of the information. Permission will invariably be needed, and possibly a fee paid, if you plan to use copyright material as part of a presentation to the public, or to an event where a fee has been charged for entry – a conference or seminar for example. Remember that photocopying can infringe two copyrights: that of the creator in the original work and that of the publisher in the typesetting. Two sets of permission will be required although usually the publisher will be able to grant both.

Copyright exists for text, letters, works of art, music, advertisements, diagrams, maps and tables, including any copyright material published on the Internet, and permission will need to be sought from either the publisher or originator of the work in question or their licensee (often the publisher). The copyright of photographs lies with the photographer unless the photo was taken during the course of the photographer's employment, and then it lies with the employer. Simply commissioning photographs does not provide for the commissioner to hold the copyright unless there is a written assignment of copyright from the photographer to the commissioner. These rules (ownership of copyright when the material is commissioned or is created in the course of employment) apply to all types of copyright material. It's also important to remember that copyright does not exist for ideas or information, but in the way the author or artist has set them down in recorded form (be it on paper, disk or audio tape). Once again, if in doubt contact the publisher of the material to find out who owns the right to license the material.

When considering reprinting articles or extracts from other publications to include in your handouts, remember the following. One of the rules of copyright is that the reproduction of a 'substantial amount' needs permission – but the definition of a 'substantial amount' can be hazy. In an attempt to clarify this, some literary bodies have agreed that extracts not exceeding certain limits may be quoted without permission, when used for the purposes of criticism and review only provided that acknowledgement to the title and author (but not the publisher, although it is an accepted courtesy to do so and useful for later readers of your book to get to the source) is made wherever the extract appears. The following limits apply:

- 400 words, as one extract, from one book
- 800 words, as various extracts, from one book, provided that no individual extract exceeds 300 words
- less than one-quarter of an article from a newspaper, journal or magazine

- less than one-quarter of a poem or a series of extracts together comprising less than one-quarter of a poem.

This agreement is known as 'fair dealing'. The following are not covered by fair dealing:

- song lyrics or music
- material to be used in anthologies
- material which has been adapted in any way from the original
- where the extract is complete in itself (an article of 350 words, for example).

However, it is important to note that this fair dealing agreement is not contained within the Copyright, Design & Patents Act 1988 (the governing legistation) and use of extracts taken under the auspices of fair dealing can be challenged by copyright holders. If in doubt, always double-check with the copyright holder.

If you do need to obtain copyright, then write to the copyright holder asking for non-exclusive permission to reproduce the desired item or extract, giving full details of the source in which you found it. Say how the item or extract is to be used (e.g. the type of publication, price and territorial distribution), and ask if a particular copyright line is required to be published each time you use it, as well as checking that the acknowledgement you plan to publish is satisfactory.

As there is often a fee involved in obtaining copyright, make an allowance for this if necessary.

Managing and writing content

Once you have identified and ordered your contents, and brought a little creativity to the process, you will feel much more confident about the next stage. You've already confirmed what you are going to say, now it's simply a matter of putting it into words – and you have probably already found that as you start to think about content the 'script' begins to write itself.

How do you plan to deliver your words?

This is the first question you need to ask yourself as, in reality, few presentations are delivered word for word from pre-written scripts. Instead you'll be relying on notes or simply remembering what you have to say.

So, the manner in which you structure the writing process does depend greatly on how you plan to deliver your words – and we'll look at the options in more detail in Chapter 4, on communication skills. But whatever you choose to do, you will still need to write down the essence of what you plan to say.

Here are a few hints on how to write for presenting, even if you don't read the end result out word for word:

- ■ You are writing to be heard not to be read: don't write long, complex sentences which your listeners will have difficulty following. Break them down into more easily absorbed sections which can be delivered (apparently) more spontaneously, and which will be easier to remember. Your ultimate aim is a conversational delivery style which appears natural and unforced.

- ■ Likewise, don't string together long lists of numbers, names or statistics. This type of detail may be better left to an accompanying visual aid or handout.

- ■ Don't use words that are obscure in meaning or are difficult to say. Your main aim is clarity, and you don't want to trip yourself up unnecessarily.

- ■ If you have to use foreign words or phrases, or words that are difficult to pronounce, write a phonetic version on your notes to help you (and practise beforehand).

- ■ Avoid jargon, acronyms or technical terms that may lose a section of your audience: if such terms have to be included, make sure they are clearly explained.

- ■ If your aim is to persuade, make sure your language reflects this by using positive words whenever possible: use 'can' not 'may' or 'could', and 'will' not 'might' and so on. A critical look at what you've written down will show up other examples. Avoid the temptation to be modest: actively adopt a more bullish tone and the end result will be much more positive.

- ■ Important points may need to be 'flagged' so that the listener knows when to listen attentively: phrases such as 'A key point is . . .' or 'Let me introduce an important point . . .'. Although this may seem very unsubtle when written down, your audience will benefit from such verbal clues to cue their attention.

■ Humour can be both the salvation and the destroyer of a presentation. Very few of us can judge the mood of an audience and deliver a joke successfully – if in doubt, leave it out. Cartoons and other illustrative material could carry humour for you, if you think it will benefit the overall presentation.

■ Anecdotes and case histories are a better way of adding interest and relevance: however, make sure the examples used are straightforward and don't require either too much background knowledge or detail (that can appear on an accompanying handout if necessary). Stick to the main points that the case study demonstrates. If you want to use the name of a third party in such material, remember to get their permission first.

■ Rhetoric adds valuable light and shade to a script, and can often be used to pre-empt the questions that are already forming in listeners' minds. If the questions you ask are 'controversial' ('So why am I telling you this', 'What's the point of all this' and variations on a similar theme), the result can be even more dynamic.

■ Prepare your handovers just as you would the rest of your presentation and include them in your notes, or remember them word for word.

■ If you are writing as a team, try to establish a basic style before you start, so that the end result remains coherent.

Starting with a bang (and ending with one too)

You've introduced yourself, the audience is settled, all eyes are focused on you. How do you keep them there? Your presentation should start with maximum impact. It should grab attention, focus thoughts and make your audience keen to hear what you have to say. How can you achieve this? Here are some suggestions:

Strike fear

Back to the poor individual presenting on pension rights. How to introduce such a potentially tedious but nevertheless vital subject? Here's an idea: a cutting taken from a newspaper that the presenter knows will be a favourite among much of his audience :

'75% of clerical workers face poverty as pension planning is neglected'

The Daily Bugle

His audience is immediately engaged – it's them he's talking about, and he's highlighted one of their greatest fears, the one they've been sweeping under the carpet. He's got them hooked – now he can tell them how to ensure a prosperous retirement, and he'll probably find they are all taking notes.

A little bit controversial?

Perhaps you've found something from your qualitative research that challenges an accepted view? Or can you think of a way of beginning your presentation that turns your audience's expectations upside down?

Tom Collins is thinking of using this quote, which came out of his telephone survey:

> 'If a modern business – of any size – doesn't know how to exploit the Internet then it won't survive.'

He might use this quote as a way of opening up a general discussion, to help his audience focus on the topic in hand and give them something to talk about.

Reassurance

You want your audience to know that you understand it. This might be a useful way of beginning a contentious presentation, or one dealing with very sensitive issues. At Crazy Crackers, Sarah Williams knows that her audience will be a rather nervous bunch of raw recruits. This is one way she could start:

> 'When I first started at Crazy Crackers, the first thing I did was to go through the door of the wrong company – the box-making plant next door. It was ten o'clock before someone found me and took me to the right place! What a way to start a career.'

Surprise

To make your audience really sit up and take notice, surprise them! You don't have to pop a balloon or run on dressed as a clown, but brainstorm other ideas that could be appropriate in your situation. Tom Collins has thought of a good trick to really engage his audience: he'll start his presentation in front of his audience and then – with the flick of a switch – continue on the computer screens placed around the room, which will be carrying a live netcast (a broadcast carried via the Internet, filmed on a digital video camera) of what he's saying.

Come on down!

Participation is a good way to open a presentation, especially if you want your audience to be relaxed and willing to contribute. Later on in this chapter we look in more detail at how you can manage audience participation, especially when opening a presentation. If you decide to kick off proceedings with a discussion or game, ensure your opening gambit can be linked logically, cleanly and emphatically to your next point. If the opening feels in any way contrived or tricksy, then the audience will become confused and lose the plot.

Closing the presentation

Your main objective, when you wrap up your presentation, is to summarize the main arguments or information you've just delivered to ensure that, if nothing else, the audience remembers those crucial salient points.

But your closing remarks don't have to end with the audience looking at a visual entitled 'Summary'. Use your imagination to make your ending more memorable.

Just as you started with impact, end with impact as well. Many of the devices used to start the show could be used to finish it: in fact one technique is to return to your opening visual or remark and then qualify it using the points you've just made in your presentation.

For example, an effective end to the pensions presentation would be a return to the opening slide:

'75% of clerical workers face poverty as pension planning is neglected'
The Daily Bugle

with the addition of a further newspaper cutting saying:

'Prudent savers expect prosperous retirement'
The Daily Comet

As we've said, many of your opening gambits can be turned into conclusions as well. You could poll the audience to see if their perceptions of an issue had changed; close with a final case history to illustrate how all the points you made can be tied together; at the very least you could end with a more creatively designed visual, to help your audience remember your final conclusion.

Presenting specific information – managing content and delivery

You may be called upon to present quite specific information, within a much tighter context. Here are a few examples, and some hints and tips on how to prepare.

Presenting statistical information

If you have to present a statistical report, then aim to deliver no more than a summary, and supply further details in accompanying handouts. Your main objective is to identify and highlight those findings of most relevance to your audience and bring out the conclusions of most importance. Your audience will not be able to remember more than a few figures at a time, and if you give them too much information you may find you have to keep repeating yourself, especially if you are inviting comparison. As a result the audience will simply feel confused.

Whatever the level of detail you decide to give, you (or your colleagues) must know the full report inside out, so that you are well armed to answer the more detailed questions that the main body of the talk will undoubtedly provoke. Visual illustrations are of great importance in such presentations and in Chapter 5 we discuss the visual presentation of figures and diagrams.

Presenting summaries of longer reports

When faced with a long and complex report, condensing it into a concise, accurate and truly representative presentation can seem very daunting. What to leave in, what to take out? Who might take offence or accuse you of misrepresentation?

A good starting point is to create an 'executive summary' covering some or all of the following points:

- The reason why the report was written.
- The main questions posed (try to summarize these into three or four overriding themes).
- The methodology used to obtain the answers.
- The key results.
- How these can be interpreted.
- The main implications of the conclusions drawn.

Already you have the bare bones of your presentation. You can of course make reference to other, interesting results that were found out along the way, but if the report is to be available to all the members of your audience then they can read the full document at their leisure. Circulate the executive summary to all those involved in preparing the full report before you present, to ensure that no noses are put out of joint.

Presenting to the media

Every so often, you may be asked to present information to journalists at a 'press conference' – perhaps to launch a new product or announce an important piece of news (a business development, for example, or the results of a survey or piece of research). For more detailed information on organizing and handling such an event, consult any book on public relations: for the purposes of this chapter, here are a few points which may come in useful when planning the presentation:

- Treat the media as an audience to be persuaded, rather than be instructed.

- Order your points as you would like to see them reported: journalists will be asking themselves 'what's the story' and then 'so what?' when assessing a piece of news.

- Depending on the nature of your audience, keep technical details to a minimum at first, and concentrate on presenting the concept: technical information can always be provided as a separate mini-presentation within the full programme, in handout material, in conversation after the event, or during the question and answer session.

- Keep the presentation short and to the point: many journalists may leave half way through, not because they are being rude but because they have deadlines to meet or have to go to another press launch on the other side of town.

- Be prepared for questions outside the context of the presentation, especially if there has been other news breaking at the same time – company results for example, or high profile resignations.

- Encapsulate your presentation in a press release. This is the handout that journalists will want, and on which they'll make notes. Make sure this is ready for them as they arrive, along with other relevant background information.

Presentations to the media can take a lot of time to prepare, and yet attract a poor turnout simply because most journalists receive three invitations for every one event they can or want to attend. A good idea is to double up a press event with a general presentation to industry guests and customers, maximizing your investment of time and money.

Presenting good or bad news

Whatever the subject matter, presenting *news* has important implications for both presenter and audience:

■ Although no one in the audience knows what you are about to say, there might have been quite a bit of gossip and second-guessing. You may want to try to get a feel for the mood of your audience before you begin, especially to ascertain if any news has been leaked.

■ Depending upon how unexpected your news is to your audience, your presentation will probably provoke quite a lot of comment: prepare yourself well and budget a generous amount of time for questions and answers. Make sure you have experienced colleagues on hand capable of answering the trickiest of questions.

■ Bad news may cause an unpleasant reaction from your audience. If you think this is likely to happen, consider the following precautions, and incorporate them into your plans. Make sure you are not presenting alone in the room – have extra assistance on hand in the venue. Bulk up your presentation team to increase your 'stage presence'. Ensure there is time and space to deal with the most enraged members of your audience away from the pressurized atmosphere of the presentation room – book an adjoining room perhaps, where you can talk more calmly and privately if necessary. Whatever the situation, don't respond to aggressive behaviour with sarcastic retorts or clever put downs: this both undermines your position, losing you the sympathy of the majority of the audience, and may enrage the aggressor even more. Make sure you have sufficient colleagues in attendance to help keep your audience under control whilst acknowledging that their emotions will be running high. Under such circumstances, question and answer sessions may get out of control – try to offer an alternative time and place for questions, when the mood is not so volatile.

■ Although presenting good news is rarely seen as a problem, presenting bad news can be far less pleasant, especially if you have been cast in the role of the 'messenger'. Even though your personal influence over the news you have to deliver is limited, mud may stick. How can you try to dilute this effect and avoid being made a scapegoat? The most practical way is to insist that a colleague closer to the decision-making process accompanies you to the presentation. Even if he or she does not say a word, make sure the audience knows that he or she is there to answer questions and make sure questions are sent in his or her direction as much as possible.

Presenter as teacher – the training presentation

Although you're not planning to become a professional training instructor, perhaps you find that from time to time, you are asked to train a group on a certain subject. What are the key elements you must remember in this context?

■ As a training presentation can take a longer time to deliver (even days), and will probably include various stages, workshop sessions or practical exercises, careful timetabling is vital. Make sure every stage receives the amount of time it deserves, and nothing is abandoned or rushed through. Give the timetable to everyone in the audience as they arrive, and run it through with them before you begin.

■ Given the longer running time, variations in style, pace and activity become vital if audience interest and attention is to be maintained. If you are faced with such a long haul, consider presenting as a 'two-hander' with a colleague in order to provide a regular contrast in style which will refresh your audience and keep things moving along.

■ Establishing the level of audience understanding is even more important in this context. Try to do this well ahead of time, perhaps by circulating a brief questionnaire to all those planning to attend, to establish the level of knowledge, and what they hope to learn from the presentation. Use their answers to pitch your presentation correctly.

■ Question and answer sessions must be inserted throughout your presentation, to ensure your audience has understood what you have said, and is ready to move on to the next point.

■ Audience participation is often very important in many training presentations. Read more on how to get the audience involved later in this chapter.

Presenting your credentials

If you work in an organization which often has to sell itself, especially if you work within the service sector, then the 'credentials' presentation may soon become a regular and important part of your marketing routine. Such presentations may seem straightforward, but the following rules are worth remembering:

■ Create a multi-purpose, interchangeable presentation that can be used in a variety of scenarios. By incorporating elements relevant to different audiences, you can quickly 'personalize' the presentation and make it appear even more appropriate. If you think it worthwhile, you could also make the presentation available in a variety of formats so that you can meet any situation as professionally as possible.

■ Avoid complacency: review and update your credentials presentation regularly to make sure you are delivering the most accurate picture of yourself or your organization. For example, check that any personnel named are still with your organization; that work samples or case histories are regularly updated; that any relevant business news is included as appropriate (perhaps you've won an award, or achieved record sales figures). Re-visiting the presentation monthly also ensures any topical issues can be incorporated (perhaps there have been legislative, political or economic changes which can be referred to).

■ No matter how many times you've done it before, rehearse what you are going to do and say before every presentation, even if it's only to yourself as you drive to the venue

■ Despite the apparently straightforward nature of your presentation, you can still start with a bang. For example

'Packaging accounts for 75% of consumer purchasing decisions'

Today's Designers

has much greater impact than:

'I am the Chief Executive of Marvellous Marketing, and I'm going to show you some of the things that our packaging division has done for our clients.'

Planning audience participation

It may seem an unnecessary extra burden, but getting the audience involved in your presentation can deliver important benefits. Audience participation can:

■ add life to the whole event, increasing understanding and appreciation of a particular point

■ provide a valuable change of pace, useful in longer or more complex presentations

■ break the ice between audience members

■ relax the atmosphere of the presentation and increase the bond between the presenter and the audience

■ encourage team building among your audience.

It's important to be fully prepared if you plan any form of audience involvement – don't assume they have all brought pens and paper with them for example, and make sure a flip chart or whiteboard is available if you need to write anything down. Depending on the estimated size of your audience you may also need help from colleagues to manage the distribution of items, collection of papers, or to answer questions from individuals as they work on an exercise.

Let's look at a few ideas for getting the audience involved:

Ice-breakers – other ways to start the show

On some occasions, you'll want to relax your audience and 'loosen it up' – perhaps if you've got a long day ahead of you, or you're relying on your audience to work together and get involved in the presentation as it progresses. An 'ice-breaker' can help stimulate your audience and get it going. Using such techniques does require a certain amount of confidence on the part of the presenter, as you'll need to guide your audience quickly, efficiently and good-humouredly through an exercise that may seem irrelevant in the wider context of the presentation you are about to give. If you feel unsure then don't try the more ambitious until your presentation skills are better honed.

Getting to know you

Ask each member of your audience to introduce themselves to the rest of the group, and to provide a little background information on themselves. If you are presenting a seminar or training session on an industry issue or skill, for example, it's useful for the audience to know where everyone is from, and useful for you to know of the experience of the group, which you may be able to draw upon as your presentation progresses.

If you feel the audience knows each other well enough already – perhaps you are presenting to a group of work colleagues – add a twist to this routine. Ask each individual to introduce themselves, give their job title, and then add a piece of information that won't be so well known to everyone else: where they were born; what they would do if they won the lottery; their favourite food/sport/colour/pop group; their star sign (even read them their horoscope from that morning's paper). Don't ask anything that might cause embarrassment or upset, and keep the emphasis light-hearted. Once again, make a mental note of any interesting answers and weave them into the following presentation.

If your audience is too large to stand up one by one, ask each individual to introduce him or herself to the person on either side, telling them their name, occupation and some other interesting fact. You could then ask who had found out the most interesting piece of information.

Games and puzzles

If you want to 'limber up' your audience, start with a few mental puzzles – look in weekend newspaper supplements, puzzle magazines or in books of brainteasers for quick ideas.

Word puzzles work well as they are quick to set up, easy to understand and need only a pen and paper, and possibly a flip chart at the front of the room. For example, pick a long word relating to the topic in hand, divide your audience into teams or groups of two, and ask them to list as many new words made up of the letters in the main word, in a minute. You could also use one of the creative thinking techniques we looked at in Chapter 2, as a game.

Physical exercises

I once attended a presentation at which the presenter started by asking every member of his (very large) audience to stand up and rub the shoulders of the person standing to their left, and then to their right! It proved a startling and memorable beginning, and helped get rid of some of the reserve that often subdues an audience comprised of professional individuals.

Asking the audience to get physically involved is better in such larger settings where self-consciousness is not so much an issue – within a group of two or three, such an activity would feel ridiculous. But if you are working with a large group, and require them to feel 'actively' involved in what you have to tell them, then asking them to stand and stretch, to loosen ties or take off jackets – and to repeat these exercise at intervals throughout your presentation if necessary – will help turn even the largest audience into a relaxed and involved group.

Survey your audience

Pose a simple, relevant question, and poll your audience for a response. Such instant surveys can be used in a number of ways:

- To get your audience thinking about a certain topic.
- To clarify expectations about the forthcoming presentation.
- To get a feel for the audience's knowledge of the topic in hand.
- To challenge assumptions, for example, by asking a question you know your audience will probably answer incorrectly.

Keep a note of the answers – perhaps on a flip chart or whiteboard – and weave the results into the subsequent presentation. As we suggested earlier, you could even return to the survey at the close, and check to see if the answers have changed.

Games and competitions

These can be used to:

- promote better understanding
- inject some humour and fun into a presentation
- give the audience a 'break'
- get an audience working in teams.

Competitive activities are more appropriate for instructive or informative business presentations, but that is not to say that such techniques need be dismissed completely when planning a persuasive presentation. The most important factor is that the competition is appropriate to the aims of the presentation, and does not seem out of context. If your audience is the right size to divide into two or three teams, then competitive games can work very well. Look at popular TV game shows for ideas, or run a straightforward general knowledge quiz, based on the subject in hand.

If a completely ridiculous game is needed – to provide light relief from solid concentration perhaps – then consider adapting some traditional party games. 'Pin the nose on the chief executive', charades and consequences, for example, can all be adapted, as can many familiar board games. Alternatively, consider some word games or mental puzzles, such as those suggested to break the ice.

And don't forget an incentive: a small prize or joke certificate can help round off the competition.

Bear in mind the following if planning a game:

- Make sure the game you choose is appropriate to the nature of the presentation, and doesn't detract from or undermine your main message.
- Place the game carefully within your overall timetable – if you are aiming to use a game as a means of relaxing your audience, use it right at the start. If your presentation demands a certain amount of concentration from your audience, use a game at the end or before a convenient break to test learning, and act as a 'treat' for working so hard.
- Make sure the person managing the game has sufficient 'presence' to organize people quickly, make things run

smoothly, and retain respect throughout the proceedings (which might turn into uproar!). If you feel you might not be able to control the group once the game is underway (especially if it is one of the more ridiculous) then consider using some other technique or share your presentation with someone else who can command the necessary authority.

- Never employ ridicule or embarrassment within a game – it will turn your audience against you.
- Keep an eye on the time and make sure your game doesn't overrun, which can easily happen. In fact, 'beat the clock' games are a good way to keep proceedings under control.

Discussion sessions

Although these often develop out of question and answer sessions, specific discussion time can be timetabled into a presentation, but it is a technique best used in informative or instructional presentations, as it can disrupt the logical flow of a persuasive presentation.

A discussion session used at the start of a presentation can be very useful:

- to reveal the expectations of an audience
- to measure the knowledge of an audience
- to establish the audience's opinions on a certain subject.

Once again, having established the above refer back to the specific points made by the audience as the presentation unfolds, making it increasingly relevant, and keeping the audience closely involved.

Used mid-way or at the end of a presentation, a discussion session can confirm understanding of key points, and expose areas of weakness. As a result, the presenter may have to go over certain points again to ensure understanding. A discussion is also a good method of introducing case history material (in this case, generated by the audience itself), as they can contribute their own experiences within the context of the topic in hand.

Managing a discussion is very similar to managing the question and answer session, which is discussed later in Chapter 4. However, it does demand more interaction from the presenter, who will have to act as both an instigator and facilitator to guide participants to a reasonable conclusion, rather than let the discussion meander on in an unfocused way.

Workshops and small group activities

Another means by which your audience can practise skills or discuss points. If you want to include such sessions within your presentation, consider the following:

- Plan carefully: don't dream up activities that are too complex or need a lot of explanation or equipment, or that will be difficult to complete in the time you have allowed.
- If you plan to hold a number of such sessions within your presentation try to make sure audience members work in different groups for each exercise, to generate different results.
- If you've planned a strict timetable then keep to it: workshops can easily overrun and force you to scrimp later on in the session. Always give your audience a 'five minute bell' so they know when to start wrapping up their work. On the same point, don't ask your audience to try to do something in too short a space of time – they'll have to rush and therefore won't be able to do the exercise properly.

Role play

Role play games are useful in the development of personal skills, as they allow an audience to put newly learnt advice into practice within a controlled and supportive environment. In some contexts, role play can prove very useful. I once attended a presentation on 'How to canvass during an election', which asked volunteers to act as bad-tempered householders opening the door on their prospective parliamentary candidate. The results were both hilarious, as the candidate gamely fought off the worst kind of questioning, and a good example of how to turn any aggressive question into a positive response!

If the subject of your presentation lends itself to role play then plan it carefully, and don't create a scenario that is too complex. If you want to limit role play to a demonstration at the front of the group then ask for volunteers, rather than select individuals at random, as you are likely to find the more extrovert members of the group (and possibly the more senior members) keener to take part. They will also be the most effective contributors and better able to handle any criticism resulting from their performance. Alternatively, divide your audience into appropriate groups, role play within the group and then share feedback afterwards with the whole audience.

Physical props

Passing a physical object around the audience can help increase the immediacy of a presentation, and may be the only way of really explaining a certain point. However, be careful how you manage such an exercise. By necessity, as an object is passed around the person examining it will not be concentrating on what you have to say. And if the audience is large, by the time the prop has reached the final member of the audience you will have moved onto another section of your presentation entirely, all the while talking over a slight disturbance caused by the object moving from hand to hand. Unless your audience is very small, and such a prop can be passed round in under five minutes, simply show such items to your audience and invite them to examine them in more detail at the end of the presentation.

Questions and answers

This is the one essential part of the presentation you can't control (although we know it must be prepared for and rehearsed in just as much detail as all the rest, and we'll look in more detail at how to handle these sessions in Chapter 4). What you *can* control is the way you place question and answer sessions into your presentation. What are the options?

At the end of the presentation

Most people expect to be able to ask questions at the end of a presentation, and it is the 'traditional' time to ask them. It is also more appropriate for those presentations which have developed a logical flow of thought, or are tying together a number of ideas into one main argument – the presentation of a sales campaign for example, or the presentation of survey results. Placing the session at the end also allows the audience to ask questions which broaden a debate, or invite digression. However, the questions asked will be in a random order, and may require the presenter to leap mentally from point to point in order to respond effectively. The session can also result in a scrappy ending to a presentation: it's therefore important to close the session properly, and add a final round-up speech to 'tidy things up'.

At regular intervals throughout the presentation

This works well when presenting a subject which comprises several 'sections', especially if your audience must understand a point fully before you can move on. Training or instructional presentations fit this bill, and also informative presentations.

If you need to incorporate frequent question sessions, then manage each session efficiently. Make sure the audience knows that only questions relating to the last section will be covered – broader questions can be kept until a final round-up session at the close, perhaps. Placing a time limit on each session is also a good way to stay in control.

Freely asked throughout the presentation

If the subject matter being covered is particularly complex, and total understanding crucial, then inviting questions as one presents will ensure no member of your audience is left behind. This can work very well and experienced presenters, who handle interruptions with ease, may even find it a better option than storing up random questions for a final session. But it can prove disruptive and really only works effectively if the audience is small. It may also require a presenter with significant 'presence' in order to control the enthusiasm of the questioners during each digression, and ensure that the focus is returned to the subject of the presentation as soon as possible.

Combining the above

Perhaps the best answer is a mix of strategies. You may even want to start off with a question and answer session to provide valuable information on audience knowledge and expectations. A mix of regular, controlled question and answer slots, followed by a concluding session at the close of the presentation will allow the audience to pick up on points that were hard to understand as they were being made, but also to address the wider issues at the end. Likewise, if you've invited your audience to ask questions freely, a round-up session is always useful in order to make sure all points have been addressed to the satisfaction of the audience.

Summary

- Begin the process of writing by listing and then ordering the points you need to make: then think creatively about how to deliver them.
- Research background and supportive material to add weight and interest to your presentation.
- Write to be heard not to be read.
- Start with a bang! And end with one too.
- Different tactics will be needed when presenting different types of information.
- One-off 'training' presentations also need a different set of tactics.
- If you need to present your credentials regularly, make your presentation responsive, flexible and easy to put together at short notice.
- Audience interaction can add life and interest to your presentation, and many different activities can be used.
- Think about the structure of your presentation, and the type of presenter you are, when planning when to schedule question and answer sessions.

Do it yourself

- You've been asked to put together a presentation on 'How to use a dictionary':
    - List and order the points you would want to make.
    - Try a creative thinking exercise and weave the results into the way you structure your content and visuals.
    - Could you get the audience involved in any way?
    - Think about any additional research you could do.
- Sarah Williams needs to think about the handout material she has to prepare for her presentation. Can you help her?

4 | COMMUNICATION SKILLS

Forget about content, attention-grabbing introductions, deal-clinching conclusions. If you mumble into your notes and don't look at the audience the whole presentation will be a disaster. This chapter looks at how to communicate what you have to say as effectively as possible.

Remembering your lines

As we noted in Chapter 3, although you may create the perfect script it's rare that you will end up 'reading it out' word for word. So how can you remember all the things you want to say – those neat little turns of phrase, those witty remarks – as you face an expectant audience?

A number of methods exist from which to choose, depending upon the type of presentation you plan to deliver.

The full script

A full transcript, word for word. When presenting, a script will need the support of a lectern large enough to hold both the pages being read and the pages already used.

When to use

- In complex presentations, requiring the delivery of detailed information which is hard to memorize or summarize.
- In certain formal situations when a 'speech' is expected, requiring perhaps a longer presentation to a larger audience.
- When presenting information that has to be delivered precisely, for example a formal statement, or information with legal implications.

Advantages

- The presentation will be delivered exactly as you planned: no points will be omitted, and elegant turns of phrase will be delivered in full.
- A greater amount of detail can be included.
- A formal atmosphere can be maintained or created.

Disadvantages

- Lack of spontaneity is inevitable unless you are very well practised in this technique. Delivery can be stilted, risking audience boredom.
- Keeping audience attention can be more difficult. Eye contact is compromised by the need to concentrate upon the script.
- If a lectern is unavailable you will have to hold the script in your hand. The result will look amateurish, and the necessary shuffling of papers can prove distracting.
- The physical handling of the script must be very professional and seamless.

How to prepare

In practical terms, a speech is best typed on smooth paper, using one side only. Number all the pages but do not join them together. Use a far larger typeface than you would when writing a normal document, as this will help you keep your place while maintaining regular eye contact with your audience. Move each page smoothly to your right when finishing – don't turn the page over.

A business speech is not the same as a rallying speech, but nevertheless it shouldn't be a drone. Consider the points made earlier on structuring a presentation script: use short sentences, avoid difficult words, where possible use interesting examples to illuminate the points you are making.

Teach Yourself Speaking on Special Occasions (Roger Mason, Hodder and Stoughton, 1996) covers speech making in more detail, and will prove helpful for anyone planning to present at a business event when a speech will be more appropriate: an after-dinner speech or a vote of thanks, for example.

Notes

Lists of key words and phrases written on separate cards, small enough to be kept in a pocket and held in the hand (index cards are a common choice).

When to use

The use of notes is acceptable in almost any presentation, except perhaps the most informal credentials presentations (when you should know everything about yourself by heart!). Most members of an audience accept the use of some form of notes, and as long as they are relatively unobtrusive they can be easily incorporated into the 'performance'. In fact, they often exist simply as a confidence booster and are, in practice, rarely used.

Advantages

■ Notes give the presenter the added confidence to deliver the presentation well.

■ They are unobtrusive and – depending upon their format – easy to hold, needing no physical support.

■ The presenter can give a more spontaneous feel to the presentation: notes allow easy interaction with both visual aids and the audience.

■ Additional points can be quickly incorporated into the running order – references to earlier speakers, for example, or to recent news, can be scribbled onto one's notes at the last moment.

■ The running order of points can also be changed quickly and easily.

Disadvantages

■ Phrasing and style have still to be memorized.

■ Notes can be dropped or get mixed up.

■ Notes can still form a barrier between the presenter and the audience, and if not used correctly can generate a stilted, robotic presentation.

How to prepare

Use small index cards or blank postcards, and use one card for each group of points (usually synchronized with your visual aids). The cards should be clearly numbered, so as to avoid confusion if they get mixed up. The level of detail you need is a very personal thing – one person might need the barest reminder of the points they are to make, while another may need to write whole sentences, especially if he or she feels they are vital to the success of the presentation. Don't be tempted to use your notes as a script, or to fill great decks of index cards. Remember they are supposed to be just a memory jogger.

When presenting as a team, handovers should be included on your notes, perhaps in a different colour ink.

Of course, in some situations notes can be far less formal, perhaps if you are presenting to one or two colleagues at very short notice. A simple list of the key points – perhaps listed on a single sheet of paper carried in a business folder or notebook (rather than on a scrappy pad) will suffice.

Presenting without *aides-mémoires*

Using memory only (prompted by information carried on any visual aids, if used).

When to use

■ 'Informal' presentations – typically internal presentations that perhaps require a complete lack of barriers between presenter and audience, or ad hoc credentials presentations.

■ Very short presentations that concentrate on a few points (which might be part of a larger presentation).

■ Presentations that are delivered regularly.

■ Presentations in which you hope to impress.

Advantages

■ Gives a highly professional appearance and earns the presenter respect (probably over and above the quality of the content).

■ Gives the presentation a very fluid, engaging quality.

■ Generates a greater feeling of spontaneity.

■ For those who work better when the stakes are high – and thrive on adrenalin – the ultimate presentation style!

Disadvantages

- If things go wrong, they will go very badly wrong. Stage fright or sudden memory loss can turn a potentially winning presentation into a complete disaster: and as a result it can increase any anxiety already felt by the presenter.
- A tendency to rely much more on visual aids as prompts: this can result in less eye contact, and is disastrous if the visual aids are obscured from view due to the layout of the room. If your display screen is placed on a boardroom table, and you have to stand alongside or even behind it, then your visual aids will be completely hidden from your line of sight.
- A lot more practice is required in order to become word perfect – there might not be enough time to prepare.
- Can appear *too* slick and well rehearsed which can in turn appear impersonal, as if you are simply reciting a familiar script and not addressing your audience directly.

How to prepare

For those of you gifted with photographic memories, learning your lines is the least of your worries, leaving you free to concentrate on delivery and style. But this will only be a lucky minority. For the majority of us, memorizing a presentation script will be fraught with worry and anxiety. But for those situations when it is absolutely necessary, the following advice can prove useful:

- Practise, practise and practise!
- You *should* know your material back to front even if you aren't word perfect when it comes to delivery. Think of your presentation as a story that you desperately need to tell someone – your enthusiasm should ensure that you remember at least the majority of key points that need to be made.
- Group the points you want to make, and co-ordinate these with your visual aids, grouping them into numbers, if it makes thing easier: for example, you know you need to make four points in the introduction, three for slide one, one for slide two, and so on.
- Your visual aids will become the prompts for your delivery, but as hinted above, don't be tempted to stand and stare at

them as you deliver your presentation. You should know your material well enough to have only to glance at the visual aid in order to remind yourself of what to say. If possible, have a copy of your visuals in front of you so that you need not turn to the screen to remind yourself of what you have to say. Overhead projector (OHP) transparencies can easily provide such cues, as they will be lit up in front of you as you present.

■ Don't panic if you realize that you have forgotten a point – given the more spontaneous feel of an 'unscripted' presentation, backtracking is much easier. And remember, your audience doesn't know that you've missed out material, only you!

■ Prepare an emergency back-up. If the worst comes to the worst and you dry up mid-flow, the knowledge that you can quickly refer to a set of notes can help save the day. However, try to keep these emergency notes to the barest minimum, condensed onto one or two cards. You don't want to add to your embarrassment by suddenly shuffling a deck of cards, trying to find your place. Alternatively, list your points on a sheet of paper and put these on a lectern or table if appropriate.

Relaxation and dealing with fear

Many people find presenting a highly stressful activity, far more stressful than most of their other work-related tasks. As a presentation approaches they find themselves exhibiting a classic 'flight or fight' response: edginess; dilated pupils; a dry mouth; rapid breathing; butterflies in the tummy; a need to visit the bathroom more often; muscle tension; sensitivity to touch; insensitivity to pain; and feeling cold.

Well, one would hope that you don't feel all these symptoms simultaneously! And it's also the case that many find such exposure to short-term stress positively beneficial: it can inspire and motivate, focus the mind and produce great bursts of channelled energy.

The ideal is obviously a balance between the two – to use stress to enhance your performance but also to remain sufficiently relaxed to gain necessary control over negative emotions. Good communication depends upon effective relaxation: a relaxed body will assume a good posture, which will in turn give rise to a controlled and calm speaking voice and a generally positive appearance. Overall, gaining such control over body and voice will boost confidence and aid relaxation.

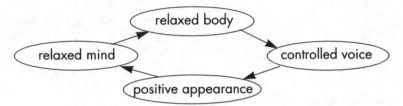

As we have said, a certain amount of tension may be no bad thing: it concentrates the mind, and helps you to 'gear up' for the moment when you enter the spotlight. After all, you don't want to become so relaxed that you appear completely laid-back and disinterested. But achieving the right balance, especially when you are still new to presenting, can be difficult. And although much advice will be handed on to you, including the ideas in this book, the best and only way to increase confidence and deal with fear is to present regularly and successfully: simply to 'get used' to the experience.

However, you may be reading this book whilst facing the first presentation of your career. So how can you help yourself relax as the big day approaches? The following suggestions should help reduce tension in the face of the big occasion.

Effective practice and thorough preparation

Practice is one of the best ways to encourage confidence: knowing your material and the way it is to be presented; feeling confident about the equipment you are to use; being prepared for the unexpected. Bear these points in mind from the outset. Book yourself extra rehearsal time if you feel you need to practise more than your colleagues, or practise at home in front of a mirror or to relatives or honest friends; practise using the equipment chosen for the day, or get some professional training if you feel you need it; talk to more experienced presenters about what happened when things went wrong, and how they got themselves out of sticky situations. Preparing a list of such anecdotes might be a useful preparation activity, another weapon in your armoury against nerves.

An important point, however, is not to over-rehearse your presentation. You run the risk of becoming bored, complacent and tired of what you have to say, and this will be apparent to your audience. Once again, keep a little edge of nervous tension to spur your performance on.

Watch what you eat and drink

Don't drink more tea or coffee than you would on a normal day, and remember that cola, cocoa and chocolate also have a relatively high caffeine content. Many people find caffeine a useful stimulant, but if you are already nervous and a little jumpy then you might find caffeine magnifies these feelings and makes you feel worse. Also remember that caffeine increases heart rate, can cause indigestion (by stimulating the production of stomach acid) and is also a diuretic – you don't want to deliver an important presentation whilst desperately needing to go to the bathroom!

Likewise, never drink alcohol to steady your nerves – the effects could be disastrous – and avoid drinking heavily the night before. Some reports state that it takes an undamaged liver an hour to deal with a single unit of alcohol. If you are presenting first thing in the morning, remember that the results of a late night drinking session may not have cleared your body by the following day. As well as the inevitable hangover, you may still be over the limit if you need to leave early to drive to your presentation venue, and black coffee, cold showers and fresh air won't sober you up. Often at conferences or other business occasions, evening socializing is an important part of the whole event, so simply be careful if you know you are presenting the same day or the following morning. You need a clear head and to be in full control of your memory and your body.

Try a proven relaxation technique

Your favourite exercise regime may include a relaxation exercise which could be adapted for use just before a presentation – many focus on relaxing various muscles of your body in turn, deep rhythmical breathing, or trying to empty your mind temporarily of thoughts that may be panicking you. You might even find that listening to a favourite piece of music as you drive to work or the presentation venue will help, or taking a short walk around the block, or simply getting some fresh air and a change of scene will help steady your nerves.

Teach Yourself Managing Stress (Terry Looker and Olga Gregson, Hodder & Stoughton, 1997) features a useful exercise that is easy to do in any situation:

Quieting reflex

- **Step One**   Close your eyes. Pinpoint in your mind what is annoying or stressing you.
- **Step Two**   Say to yourself: 'Alert mind, calm body. I'm not going to let this get to me.'
- **Step Three**   Smile to yourself. You can practise smiling to yourself without showing a smile on your face. In this way your smile will not be obvious to others around you.
- **Step Four**   Breathe in to the count of three, while imagining that the air comes in through holes in your feet. Feel the sensation of warmth and heaviness flowing throughout your body, starting at your feet and ending at your head.
- **Step Five**   Breathe out to the count of three. Visualize your breath passing through your body from your head and out through the holes in your feet. Feel the warmth and heaviness flow through your body. Let your muscles relax, let the jaw, tongue and shoulders go limp.

    Now open your eyes and resume your normal activity.

Authors Terry Looker and Olga Gregson say that with several months of practice, this exercise can quickly promote an automatic feeling of relaxation.

Visualization

This is another technique which needs to be practised over a longer period of time. Visualize an image which you associate with calm, relaxing thoughts – it might be a favourite holiday spot, or the sea, a meadow, a sunset. Prior to the presentation, take a few minutes to sit quietly, close your eyes and bring this image into your mind and relax as you visualize the picture. This technique needs to be practised first, to build up your positive relaxed reaction to the image you choose.

Voice control and delivery style

When presenting your aim is to be as clear as possible, as engaging as possible, to project as much enthusiasm/commitment/concern as possible and yet still appear as 'natural' as possible. Good voice control will help you achieve this. Remember the following advice, and practise it when you rehearse:

- Speak slightly more slowly than you would in everyday speech, and with more clarity. Enunciate words carefully, and lower the volume of your voice as you end each sentence (but not to such an extent that your audience must strain to hear you).

- Don't drop your head when you speak, but keep it tilted up. This will help voice projection.

- Vary the pitch and tone of your voice as you speak: a well-structured presentation will help you achieve this by varying the way the material is delivered. You can also practise some more 'natural' phrases to help you, such as 'Now let's take a look at . . .', 'I'm sure you'll agree that . . .', 'How best to explain . . .'. Such turns of phrase make for a more engaging and natural delivery and help you achieve the desired conversational style.

- Don't forget to pause! You may want to create a dramatic effect, but you also want your audience to absorb information before you move on. There's always the danger of rushing your words, due to nerves, and keeping talking due to a fear of silence – keep calm, slow down and give your audience a chance!

- If enthusiasm is required then practise speaking in an actively enthusiastic and committed way – emphasize those words or phrases that are really important, and use body language to underline the points you are making (see the section later on in this chapter for more on this topic).

- If using a microphone, practise first before you present, in the venue if at all possible, to gauge the correct volume of voice needed, and to let your ear adjust to the placement and sound of the speaker system used.

- If you're not using amplification, practise talking in a voice loud enough to reach all parts of your audience, especially if the venue is large. Once again, practise in the venue if at all possible, or alternatively in a room of a similar size. Remember that a room full of people will absorb sound so don't be fooled by the echoes of an empty auditorium.

■ Avoid theatricality. Some – and some may say the best – presenters are unashamedly theatrical. Their presentations are in turn amusing, enthralling, filled with emotion and import and will always make an impression on the audience. But such presentations are also usually the result of years of practice, experience and review and depend greatly upon the unique charisma of the presenter.

■ If your mouth tends to dry up when speaking, try to ensure a glass of water is placed discreetly near your speaking station.

■ If you are presenting in a team, go through the same exercises to establish volume and so on, but do it together. Try to attain an even, balanced 'sound' across the team, whilst maintaining individual characteristics which will add interest to the presentation.

■ Use a tape recorder to practise your technique. Listen to yourself simply reading a section from your presentation, and then think how you could improve it. Simply by changing the tone of your voice, increasing the vocal light and shade of your speech, you can immediately produce a more engaging result. Listen to presenters on TV or radio and analyze how they make their words sound interesting.

■ If you have a strong regional accent, make sure that you will be understood by all members of your audience. Don't think that you have to hide or disguise your accent, but you may need to temper it slightly in order to ensure maximum understanding.

Body language

The growing awareness of body language indicates just how important a factor this has become in business. When thinking about body language, remember that your overriding objective is to ensure the audience listens to what you have to say, and is not distracted by the way you are saying it, consciously or subconsciously.

Do you have any irritating, repetitive mannerisms or visual tics which must be controlled? Do you wave your hands around too much when you talk? Do you maintain a pleasant expression throughout the presentation, or do you grin like a mad monkey when not frowning at your shoes? (You might also find that verbal tics have crept into your performance: do you start every sentence with 'Well . . .' and introduce every visual with 'As you can see . . .'?)

Unconscious though they may be, such mannerisms detract from a performance: the audience will start to notice the way you tilt your head or thrust forward your jaw when making an important point, instead of listening to your words.

The best way to identify such mannerisms is to video yourself and watch the result closely. A word of warning: most people find watching a video of themselves excruciatingly embarrassing, especially if it is in the company of colleagues. Get past the cringing stage as quickly as you can – it is not vanity that makes you examine your performance in such detail, but an attempt to take the viewpoint of the audience. Getting your colleagues to view and criticize your performance will also prove useful (and undoubtedly character building!).

When thinking about body language during a presentation, here are some basic rules.

Remember to smile

Try to adopt a 'pleasant' expression throughout the presentation, smiling frequently as appropriate – it's easy to look very serious when presenting, and even to actively frown when concentrating hard. A smile works wonders in lifting an atmosphere and relaxing the audience.

Adapt your body language to suit the situation

Nerves will make you physically tense: you'll stand awkwardly, want to cross your arms or fidget. Actively adopt a 'neutral' pose whenever possible: stand upright and tall, let your arms hang loosely at your sides, or lightly hold your notes and make any gestures confidently and with purpose. If the presentation is a formal event, then you need to reflect this in your confident, poised appearance and demeanour; however, if the presentation is less formal – you want to encourage audience participation, for example, and actively break down the barriers between presenter and audience – a more relaxed style may be appropriate. You could lean against a table when you talk, for example, walk around more, or adopt a more 'natural' stance, as if you were taking part in a conversation.

Move slightly while you talk

This adds animation, which might sound odd, but consider the impression you will make if you stand stock still for the entire duration of your talk. Lean or move towards the audience as you make important points and don't back away, especially during the question and answer session.

Even if you are sitting for your entire presentation – a portfolio presentation for example, or a one-to-one presentation within a small room – your body language is still important. Lean forward to promote enthusiasm and interest. Avoid those irritating mannerisms. Don't be tempted to shuffle or play with any papers or pens that may be within easy reach, or to doodle or scribble.

Enter the room with a confident gait, good posture and a purposeful appearance – it all contributes to the final impression.

Eye contact

Eye contact is a crucial factor for the success of any presentation, as it increases the relevance and impact of what you are saying. Remember the following:

- As you begin your presentation, make direct eye contact with as many people as possible.
- Don't hide behind notes, presentation equipment, lecterns or other props that you may have with you whilst you present. Tempting though it will be to use such items as physical or psychological support, they also present a barrier between you and your audience, lessening the impact of what you have to say. Overcome this by maintaining eye contact.
- When using visual aids, don't stare at them while describing them or talking about them in your script. Of course, you will have to make reference to them, and even physically point things out, but remember to address your comments to your audience, who don't want to stare at the back of your head.
- If you are presenting to a larger audience, say of 20 or more people, mentally define a loose triangle and move your gaze from point to point, avoiding one individual (or he or she will start to feel very uncomfortable) and covering the group as a whole. If certain individuals have raised points, or you know they are interested in particular sections of the

presentation, then make eye (and verbal) contact to emphasize those particular points, and show you have remembered their question.

Communicating as a team

Team presenters have to deal with two further communication issues: how to hand over while presenting; and what to do when not presenting.

Handovers

Team presentations must remain smooth and fluid, especially when the baton is passed from one presenter to the next. Handovers can be handled in two ways: by a central presenter who introduces the presentation, introduces each presenter, and then concludes; or by each presenter handing on to the next. The latter scenario is probably the more common, but it is a good idea to open and close with the same presenter (perhaps the most senior member of the group, or the team leader), in order to provide a sense of completion.

Any handovers *must not be ad libbed*. Even though they should appear natural and unforced, they must be planned as carefully as every other part of the presentation: in fact they can be used to emphasize key points, another reason why they should not be neglected

Handovers must be practised until they become as smooth as possible, and even though they are scripted, they should be committed to memory. Exceptions to this rule include the introduction of speakers who need a more formal description, perhaps including a career summary or other details.

When handing over, look at the next presenter for part of the handover, to emphasize the change in team. The new presenter can then pick up on an earlier point to help move the presentation on.

Let's look at some of the handovers the Marvellous Marketing team has scripted:

(Jane to Fergus)

'. . . we'll now look in more detail at our analysis of Industrial Instruments' strategy in the European arena, and so I'll hand over to our export specialist, Fergus Davis, who has particular experience of this field . . .'

'. . . Thank you Jane. Just to pick up on that last point, cost-effective marketing is especially important in an international campaign, as resources can be spread quite thinly over a wide geographical area . . .'

(Fergus to Pauline)

'I'd now like to hand over to our Managing Director, Pauline Palmer, who'll summarize the reasons why Marvellous Marketing will be able to deliver the campaign Industrial Instruments needs . . .'

'Thank you Fergus – and as I'm sure you'll need more time to consider the points Fergus has just raised there, may I remind you that all the information we've covered today is fully detailed in the proposal document we've brought with us. So, why use Marvellous Marketing? . . .'

(Pauline passing back to Jane)

'So, to conclude our presentation, I'll ask Jane to sum up what we consider to be the main challenges facing Industrial Instruments, and the way we plan to respond to those challenges. Jane . . .'

Seating a team

Arrange all your seating at one side of any screens or display equipment that may be used, and close to any lecterns or tables. This will avoid crossing any visual images that may be showing when a handover takes place. Curving the seating slightly will soften the impression given by a wall of presenters, and will also reduce the distance each has to walk to reach the presentation 'station'. Always remember to have enough chairs for *all* members of the presentation team, or else someone will be left standing at question and answer time.

What to do when not presenting

It's very difficult not to feel a bit left out when not presenting, and to forget that you are still being watched. A negative or bored expression, a look of relief when your turn is over, or a slouched or relaxed pose will be noticed by the audience and will reflect badly on your entire team. Likewise, don't let your body betray your nerves: are your ankles and legs crossed and your arms tightly folded?

Whilst sitting down remain alert, interested and supportive. Sit neatly, hands held loosely in your lap, but try to avoid sitting in an identical fashion to your neighbour. Look at the presenter and appear interested and engaged in what is being said; adopt a pleasant, half-smiling expression; nod at crucial points and laugh or smile at any jokes. Acting in such a way may feel even more peculiar than just sitting still and keeping one's head down, but it is amazing what a difference it makes. Video your team in practice. You'll see how an actively interested and supportive team positively contributes to the whole presentation.

Handling question and answer sessions

Nearly all presentations will prompt questions from the audience. Usually this is a good sign – your audience has been listening to what you have to say, and is keen to debate certain points or to ask for further information. Sometimes the presenter may be dreading the questions that a presentation will prompt, but if this is the case then the questions must be easy to predict and therefore to prepare for.

And this is the key to a successful question and answer session – preparation. Although obviously much more spontaneous, the session must still be carefully managed: both in the way the audience is allowed to participate, and how responses are given to the questions asked.

Managing and controlling question and answer sessions

In Chapter 3 we looked at how to schedule questions and answers. Now we'll look at how to use your communication skills to manage them effectively.

You don't want a question and answer session to become messy and incoherent. Consider the following issues:

Who will answer the questions?

If you are presenting alone, then the answer seems fairly obvious, but if you think you may be asked questions on subjects beyond your knowledge, consider asking a colleague to come along to provide back-up. It might even be the case, if a tricky question is asked, that another member of the audience could answer it better than you can! If it feels right, don't feel embarrassed about involving the audience in such a way – perhaps not to baldly solicit an answer but to ask for an opinion or invite a comment, especially if you know there is an expert in the room. This will add life to the whole event.

If you are part of a presentation team, then one option is to designate a team member to 'chair' the question and answer session – probably the team leader. It will be up to him or her to invite questions and nominate respondents. Although the person chosen for this job may be a senior member of the team, it is important that all team members are involved in answering questions, to show that all are knowledgeable on the subject in hand, so the team leader must ensure questions are evenly distributed in order to achieve a good balance. Once a question is 'in debate' then all team members can contribute if it seems appropriate, but do restrain from pitching in all at once, or from prolonging the debate unnecessarily.

Can everyone hear the questions?

This may become a problem if you are presenting in a large auditorium, or to a large group of people. If you are already using amplification on the platform, one solution is to use a 'roving mike', as used by chat show hosts when they descend on their audience. A cordless microphone can be passed to individual members of the audience when they want to speak, managed by a member of the presentation team or an assistant: you may need more than one microphone if the audience is large.

Answering difficult questions

Even though you will have rehearsed all the likely questions you can think of time and time again, you will still be asked questions which you can't answer. How do you respond in such situations? Here are a few useful hints to remember in an emergency (if you can't remember the answer to a question, at the very least don't forget the following!). So, what do you do when . . .?

You don't know the answer

Honesty is the best policy: if you really don't know the answer, don't pretend you do. However, don't simply refuse to answer the question. Try a reply such as:

> 'That's a very interesting question, and I'm sorry, but I don't know the answer. I can find out for you. If I could take your card after the presentation, I can forward the information to you.'

or

> 'That's a very good question, and I'm sorry, I don't know the answer. I obviously need to do some more research. Can I get back to you when I've found out more?'

This might also be an opportunity to throw the question to the floor, along the lines of:

> 'I've never come across that particular problem before – has anyone here had a similar experience, and if so how did they tackle it?'

You don't understand the question

Some questioners seem incapable of phrasing a comprehensible question, and it's easy to panic in the face of a long and rambling diatribe with no apparent point. If this happens, thank the questioner for their question, then pick out what you understand to be the key points, rephrasing the question in your own words and inviting the questioner to verify. If you had difficulty understanding the questioner, it is highly likely the audience did as well – rephrasing the question avoids embarrassing the incoherent questioner, and may also allow you to make the question easier to handle.

The question requires a very detailed answer

If the question is of interest only to a small section of the audience – a technical query for example – the best option is probably to say:

> 'Thank you for that question. To do it justice I would have to go into some detail – perhaps if we could talk after the presentation, then I can give you all the information you require?'

Ask if other audience members would like the same information – if they would then it's appropriate to give a fuller answer at this point.

The question addresses some basic point you thought was already understood

A question of this kind can come as a surprise, particularly if you had already given the answer as a main point of the presentation. It might be worth politely enquiring if the rest of the audience had found this particular point difficult to understand. If they all say yes, then you may need to go over that section of your presentation again. If the majority say no, then provide a briefer answer and offer to meet the questioner after the presentation to cover the same ground in more detail. Invite other members of the audience to join in if they would like to.

The questioner becomes aggressive

You may have had to give a presentation in a volatile atmosphere – perhaps at a shareholders' meeting – or you've had to address staff on a difficult issue, matters of redundancy, for example.

It's even more important, in such a situation, to rehearse all possible answers in order to feel fully prepared and to give you the confidence to reply to heated questioning. Look back at the earlier section on delivering bad news, and remember the points made there: make sure you have colleagues present who can provide back-up; if possible, take the questioner to one side, or to a neutral situation, where the atmosphere may be less heated; and don't be tempted to reply to aggressive questioners with 'clever-clever' comments.

If your aggressive questioner asks difficult questions, then another tactic can be employed. Listen to politicians being interviewed, and note how they avoid addressing particularly thorny issues by constantly referring back to their main point or the issue at stake, starting their reply by saying:

> 'That's a very interesting question, but can I first remind you that . . .'

or

> 'I'm glad you've raised that point because it refers back to the point I made earlier . . .'

This technique must be used sparingly, as it can easily antagonize the questioner. Use it more as a way of gathering your thoughts and taking a deep mental breath while you work out how to deal with the nub of the question raised.

Non-verbal communication: personal presentation

As we've already noted, whenever you present, you are the centre of everyone's attention, no matter how informal the context. When under such direct and unwavering scrutiny, personal presentation can greatly influence the impression you make on your audience, and can impact significantly on what you have to say.

Inappropriate appearance sends confusing messages

To take an extreme example, if you turned up to present a major report to your company's board of directors dressed in jeans and a T-shirt, the impression you'd make would be one of disrespect or poor judgement: probably exactly the opposite of what you want to achieve. Of course, you would never do such a thing (we hope) but even a slightly inappropriate 'look' can take away from what you are trying to achieve. Whatever you wear, you'll be making a statement and this statement becomes exaggerated in the hothouse atmosphere of a presentation room. However, as we will see it is also important to dress 'appropriately' for the occasion: in certain cases, jeans and a T-shirt may be far more fitting than a formal outfit.

People should not be distracted by your appearance

Following on from the point above, you may be wearing the most expensive, best tailored suit in the room, but if it is a vintage 1970s model, complete with flared trousers and kipper tie, then your appearance will actively distract your audience, and their memory of the presentation may be your amazing suit, not what you had to say! Your main aim is to make your audience focus on the presentation and not on your appearance.

Dressing with care shows respect for your audience

After all, you are demanding their attention and their time and you want them to listen to what you have to say. Dressing well (and again, appropriately) shows that you have thought carefully about *all* aspects of your presentation and are keen to make a good impression.

Feeling comfortable will make you more relaxed

We have all experienced the feeling of being over or underdressed at a social gathering, and spending the entire time wishing we were wearing something else. Well don't let it happen at a presentation. If you are dressed appropriately then you can forget about your appearance, relax and concentrate on the job in hand.

What to wear?

Your most successful presentation outfit will be the most appropriate to the situation and the most comfortable to wear (both physically and psychologically) as it's not always the case that a smart appearance is necessary.

Run through a quick checklist to help you decide:

Is the presentation formal or informal?

A formal presentation is easy to dress for – simply choose your 'best' business outfit (and we'll see later in the chapter how to make sure your best outfit is working with you rather than against you).

But planning an outfit for an informal presentation can be quite difficult – you don't want to appear overdressed, yet you don't want to appear so casual that no one respects what you are saying. And no matter how informal the presentation may be, it is still an 'occasion' and one in which you are demanding attention. Toned down formality is probably the most appropriate: a shirt and tie, leaving the jacket behind; skirt or smart trousers and blouse.

Is the presentation in-house or external?

If presenting externally then you and your personal appearance will reflect the organization you represent, and so it's even more important to get it right. Does your company have a dress code? If it does, this will guide your choice of outfit: if not, should one be introduced to make life easier for everyone?

Over the years, certain professions have adopted certain styles of dress. Professional services, such as lawyers, bankers and so on tend towards traditional 'sober' outfits; creative people want to appear independently minded and fashionable. It's difficult to generalize and, of course, wheels within wheels do exist: lawyers aiming to find business within the music industry may find they need a more contemporary image; designers working for traditional companies may need to dress more conservatively.

The key is to try to predict the audience's own values and expectations and match them, without disguising your own identity too much. Are you expected to appear sober and responsible? Or wacky and inventive? Assess this and adapt your whole style to suit.

On the other hand, you may want to relax the audience by your style of dress. Should Bill Bailey of Crazy Crackers wear his 'Mr Tickle' tie to put his new recruits at ease? Probably not if he wants to retain their respect, but perhaps Tom Collins could go for an open-necked shirt and smart trousers rather than a formal suit, to help establish a more relaxed atmosphere.

Is personal style important?

Personal politics plays a major role in what you choose to wear, and you may naturally rebel against conservative, formal business dress. But, and not to repeat the point endlessly, the presentation is not about you. It's about what you are saying. Your personal appearance should support this, and not distract from it. Remember, whatever you wear makes a statement about you. If you decide not to compromise and wear whatever you want, then don't be surprised if the audience refuses to compromise its viewpoint, prejudices or stereotypical expectations – however you want to describe it.

You'll probably end up compromising whether you like it or not. You might want to appear a trendy, creative and imaginative young thing because that's what you are, but you might also want to appear capable of handling a major contract for a large amount of money. Choose your outfit with extra care, and with the expectations of your audience clearly in your mind. If they themselves are paragons of fashion, then a more outré style will be acceptable; but if you are presenting your business plan to a group of potential investors, be more conservative.

Are there any practical considerations to take into account?

Run through the following:

- Do you have to travel to the presentation? If you have to change trains or walk a certain distance, then high heels or shoes that pinch will do you no favours. If you have to drive, wear driving shoes whilst travelling (although make sure you change them before you get out of your car) and take your coat or jacket off to avoid creases. Don't ignore the weather even if you're travelling by car – a dash across a wet car park could ruin your appearance, so take a coat and umbrella if the forecast is for rain.

■ Will you need to carry or set up equipment on your own? If any form of physical activity is required, choose an outfit that allows ease of movement; avoid skirts or shirts that are too tight or heels that are too high to walk in easily, especially when carrying weighty equipment. Trouser suits and trousers for women, are becoming more acceptable as a form of business dress, but unfortunately they are still regarded as less formal than a skirt. However, they are more practical if you have to set up a complex presentation alone, and your audience will hopefully make allowances for that. If possible, set up wearing casual clothes and change before the presentation begins. This may be feasible if you are presenting in a venue such as a hotel, but might be too much to ask if presenting in the office of a potential customer!

■ Are you presenting outdoors? You may have to take your audience with you and present around a building site, in a muddy field, or at a roadside – locations in which a business suit and smart shoes would become an instant liability. You can still dress appropriately, but as smartly and as cleanly as possible. Most people would consider you sensible, level-headed and therefore worth listening to if you arrive clad in rubber boots (clean of course) and a rain jacket for a presentation starting in a farmyard – and not if you arrive in six inch heels and a mini skirt.

Are you presenting alone or in a team?

Team presentations bring the added dimension of group appearance, and so it's important that all team members agree in advance on what to wear in order to avoid any unfortunate clashes, or similarities. A group of women all presenting in different shades of purple may look very odd! In truth, women need to think this through more carefully than men, as a much broader range of colours and styles are available. Female presenters should try to ensure that they are wearing colours that at least complement, and styles that are similar. In the case of men, although the choice and variety of suit styling has greatly increased over recent years, in reality most men opt for a neutral, dark colour, perhaps choosing a lighter shade for summer or less formal occasions. However, guard against displaying a clashing group of ties or socks, or all wearing the same basic tie. The end result would appear very strange!

Personal grooming

Once your basic outfit has been decided, don't neglect your personal grooming.

Personal hygiene

All this should be obvious: bathe or shower on the day of the presentation, wash your hair and brush your teeth, use deodorant, perfume and so on. Make sure fingernails are clean and neat. Take combs, brushes, breath fresheners with you and if your presentation doesn't start until late in the working day, pack your toothbrush and toothpaste along with other essentials and make sure you freshen up before you begin.

Business accessories

Look at your briefcase, handbag, document wallet or other business accessories and make sure they are as presentable as possible. Check *all* aspects of your business accessories: don't open an expensive document wallet to reveal a cheap pen, or keep documents in tatty folders within your smart briefcase. The smallest details are often the easiest to correct, yet if left unremedied can undermine a carefully assembled appearance. If you need to buy new business accessories, make sure you buy the best you can afford.

Personal accessories

Check the state of your presentation shoes. Always make sure they are polished and clean, and do not need reheeling. Wear an older pair for driving (see above) to prevent shoes wearing at the back of the heel. Socks and tights must, of course, be without holes or snags: women should always pack an extra pair of tights in case of last-minute disasters.

Jewellery must be discreet and appropriate, clean and well made. Avoid clanking bracelets or dangling earrings – any form of jewellery that has a life of its own once you start to move, as it can prove quite distracting for the audience. And remember to change your colourful watch for a more discreet model if necessary. Male jewellery, such as an earring, can still cause offence to a more conservative audience, so if in doubt leave it out.

Make-up

This is an area of personal taste, and although statistics may show that women who wear make-up are more successful, if it makes you feel uncomfortable then don't change now. Most women have established a beauty routine that suits them and their faces, but that's not to say you should not be open to new ideas: many department stores offer mini 'make-overs' within their cosmetic departments, and it could be worth booking a session and trying out new shades or new products.

Colour analysis

The popularity of 'power dressing' and 'dressing for success' has given rise to the colour or image consultant. Don't dismiss their services as being a waste of money. If you present frequently, or are in a job where personal presentation and image are important, then a session or two may prove very useful.

Colour and image analysis tries to define what really suits you by looking at your physical shape and your skin and hair colour. A first step is to define your body shape. This enables you to identify those styles which are more flattering than others, and those styles to avoid. The next stage is to analyze the colours and shades that suit your skin tone and hair colour: the end result is a blueprint for your business wear.

As you can probably tell, there is often little room for high fashion in such a regime (although looking 'contemporary' is important), and some may feel that the end result is a characterless business outfit that hides their true personality. But for most the principles of image analysis can prove a useful guide. After all, few can afford to buy a new business outfit every time the occasion demands it: the sensible approach is to buy one or two outfits that can be interchanged, and to buy the best quality possible. It's unlikely that you'll buy clothes so fashionable that they will only last a season (unless of course, fashion is your industry) – you'll go for something that looks good but will last a number of years. The conclusions of an image analysis will help you do that with greater accuracy and far smaller risk of making an expensive mistake.

A number of organizations offer image analysis, especially tailored for business men and women: a cheaper alternative is to buy or borrow one of the many books written on the subject and see what you think.

Creating a presentation wardrobe

If you are presenting even semi-regularly it's important to build up a small wardrobe of items you feel comfortable wearing in any given situation. To get you started, the following basic guidelines may prove useful when narrowing down your choices.

Darker colours carry more authority

If you can only afford one suit, opt for a darker neutral that suits your age and colouring – black, dark grey, navy or dark brown, for example. It can easily be brightened up with scarves, ties, jewellery or other accessories as the occasion demands.

Avoid clutter

This is especially important around the head area where you hope attention will be focused. Outfits with fussy necklines, bow ties or ties that are too bright, dangling jewellery or complicated scarves can detract from your face and therefore your words.

Socks

Men take note: your socks will be revealed as soon as you sit down. Make sure they match your suit (and each other), are clean and without holes, and avoid humorous or unusual designs which might draw attention (especially those musical socks you got for Christmas). Buy a pair specifically to wear with your presentation suit: and make sure they are long enough. You don't want to reveal an expanse of unattractive hairy white calf if you sit down and cross your legs.

Aim to look contemporary, if you don't want to be fashionable

Not all of us can afford to change our best suit twice a year to match the latest catwalk trends. But that doesn't mean to say that an outfit has to remain boringly traditional: nor should it be worn if the style is truly out of date (remember that 1970s suit). Changing your accessories is the easiest way to update an outfit: this season's fashionable colour can be reflected in a scarf or tie, as can a current design trend or style. It's far easier (and more economical) to change your blouse, shirt or shoes with the seasons than replace your whole wardrobe.

Spending wisely

Being told to buy the best you can afford always seems rather wishy-washy advice. Isn't it rather a case of how much you *want* to spend? Business wardrobes are expensive investments, but consider how many times you will be wearing what you buy. If you invested in two good suits and an additional jacket and skirt/trouser combination, those three main purchases, along with shirts/tops/shoes, and so on, could last you at least two business years, especially if you change the accessories to match the trend in fashion as advised above. In fact, a very good suit could give four or five years' wear if treated properly, resulting in excellent value for money.

Sales can prove a happy hunting ground for the presenter on a budget or otherwise. Concentrate on looking for specific items and don't be influenced by 'amazing' reductions on inappropriate clothes. High-priced items such as jackets, suits and overcoats are often good buys at sale time, but concentrate on those styles and colours which will last for longer than the current season.

Another good tip is to look out for business clothes that can be machine washed: they will cut your dry cleaning bills considerably.

Summary

■ Choose an appropriate method of remembering your words: one which both works in the context of your presentation, and with which you feel comfortable.

■ Stay relaxed: prepare well, watch what you eat and drink and if you know you'll be nervous, practise a relaxation technique.

■ Aim to control your voice so that you speak at the correct speed and volume, and with a conversational style.

■ Avoid irritating mannerisms and verbal tics: adopt positive body language and maintain eye contact.

■ Teams need to practise handovers until they are word perfect. They must also practise what to do when not presenting.

■ Practise managing question and answer sessions, including how to answer difficult questions, before you present.

■ Personal presentation is an important form of non-verbal communication, and so should not be neglected when you plan your presentation

Do it yourself

■ How should each of our presenters prepare their notes? When should they schedule their question and answer sessions?

■ Write a relaxation checklist to keep in your pocket, to refer to in times of stress.

■ Let's imagine that this chapter represents the content of a presentation which will be delivered by a team of three. Write handovers for the first four sections of this chapter.

■ List your current presentation wardrobe, then write yourself a shopping list. Have fun!

5 | ILLUSTRATING YOUR PRESENTATION

Few presenters can – or want – to hold the attention of the audience by the power of words alone. Most presenters use visual, and sometimes audio, aids to illustrate and emphasize the points they want to make and to add variety and interest to the whole event.

In Chapter 2 we looked at how to start planning your visual presentation. In this chapter we look at how to put together visual material, and how to present it: how to inject style and creativity into your visual material; and how to handle the presentation equipment you choose to use.

Creating visual aids

Once the structure of your presentation has been established, and the order of points decided, you can start to plan your visual aids. Start the process by taking a broad view:

- What are the most important points, and where do they occur in the running order?
- Does any specific information need a specific visual – a graph, diagram or photograph for example?
- Can you use visual aids to add interest, excitement or humour to your presentation?
- What visual 'statement' do you want to make?
- Will sound or video add interest to the presentation, or help clarify or illustrate a point?

The answers these questions generate will provide your basic plan: you'll know the information that needs to be illustrated, roughly what type of illustrative material will be appropriate, and you'll have an idea of the style in which you want to present it. I don't think there is any golden rule about how many visuals per minute, or per presentation: the number of visuals you produce will be governed by the nature of the material you are presenting. But it is a good idea to keep the flow of visuals reasonably regular and evenly paced: you don't want to move on to a new section of the presentation whilst a list of points from the previous section remains in view.

So what can you use to create a suitably informative and engaging audio-visual display?

Words

Key words, key phrases, key points, key quotes: these can provide effective illustrative material, even when used on their own. Quick and simple to create, a visual presentation based solely on text can be prepared at very short notice, and yet still look professional, thanks to the sophistication of current word processor, DTP and presentation software. A golden rule: keep any wording short and succinct, and double-check spelling and grammar (see pages 121–3 for more on this).

Pictures

Cartoons, logos, photos, drawings – any form of illustration. A number of factors will determine how best to use pictures:

- Subject matter – does it lend itself to the use of illustrations?
- Time – gathering together or preparing illustrations may take longer than you can afford, especially if you've been asked to present at very short notice.
- Budget – can you afford to commission illustrative material or will you have to hunt around for something appropriate that already exists? If this is the case, don't forget the copyright laws.
- Is a strong visual image part of your organization's 'persona'? For example, if you represent a graphic design or advertising agency then your visual display will be an important method of representing the creativity of your company, and will be worth spending more time and money creating.

When considering illustrations, also remember the following:

Cartoons

Even if they aren't hilariously funny, cartoons can provide a safe way of injecting humour. They can open or close a presentation on a high note, and can act as a useful filler between points, as long as the presentation is one in which humour will be welcomed.

It's most likely that you will have seen the cartoon you want to use already published in a magazine or newspaper. If you want to reproduce it for a presentation, then once again remember the copyright laws. An alternative – if you have the budget – is to commission your own. Professional cartoonists can be found in any trade telephone directory (usually within the Commercial Artists section) and the result will, of course, be directly relevant to the subject matter in hand. Once again, this is an expense to include in your budget, but if you are hoping to win or retain a major contract, or are planning a presentation which is to be used many times, then it may be worth considering.

Photos

Photos reproduce well as slides and on computer-generated presentations, but not so well on OHPs, so remember your presentation medium when deciding how to use photography. If the quality of the photographic image is important – if you want to show examples of artwork, package design and so on – then 35 mm slides remain the best medium for producing crisp, sharp, colourful images.

If you are planning to use a PC to present your visuals, then it's worth considering a digital camera. These are getting cheaper all the time and they allow you to take photos just as you would with a 'normal' camera, and then download the photographs directly into your PC for further manipulation and reproduction.

Figures and diagrams

If you are presenting statistical information or facts and figures then a diagram, graph or other appropriate visual will greatly improve understanding. You can also show a much wider range of information than perhaps you could cover verbally, and if copies of these visuals are included in your handouts, then your audience can examine them in more detail after the presentation.

But don't just draw up a neat graph or pie chart: let your imagination take you further. For inspiration, watch any TV news or current affairs programme, or look at a daily newspaper: programme makers and editors almost always present statistical results using innovative, imaginative design, improving both appearance and understanding. Even though they have the benefit of sophisticated software, you can still employ the general principles when creating your visuals. For example:

- Use an illustration as a backdrop when showing simple figures such as graphs or pie charts. The Crazy Cracker team could use money bags or calculators perhaps, when it comes to showing financial information.

- Use unusual images in place of traditional alternatives. Marvellous Marketing plan to use a bar chart which shows the comparative export success of a number of different companies, but instead of simply shading each bar, they're going to use a repeat pattern, based on the logos of each company.

- Physical props can illustrate statistical information effectively, and can add a new dimension to understanding, especially if audience interaction becomes part of the presentation. For example, to illustrate the fast pace of change in the Crazy Cracker Accounts Department, Bill Bailey decides to bring an old comptometer machine to his presentation, and put it next to a modern calculator.

Audio and video clips

The growing sophistication of PC-based presentation technology makes the use of sound and motion increasingly common, and also allows its seamless introduction into the flow of the presentation, and we'll look at this in more detail later in this chapter. But for those of us with less sophisticated technology to hand (or less experience in using it) the more familiar tools of the tape recorder, television and VCR can still be used to good effect.

Audio and video, used appropriately, will add interest and life and provide a welcome change of pace and focus – and a rest for the presenter! If you plan to introduce music or the spoken word into your presentation, make sure your equipment is suitable for the job; that any loudspeakers are loud enough for all the audience to hear without distortion; that the TV screen is large enough for your audience to view; that you have enough power points to support all the extra equipment you plan to use.

Make absolutely sure that your video or audio tape is cued up for immediate use: you don't want to mess about with a tape recorder or VCR remote control, trying to find your place, and ruin the flow of your presentation. If you need to use a number of different video or audio clips, put each one on a separate tape and make sure each is clearly labelled and ready to use.

A final point: make sure you know what to do with yourself whilst running a tape. If it's a video, then it's simple enough to join the audience and watch; if it's an audio tape, then you'll have to remain at the front of the room. Make sure you maintain that pleasant, interested expression you've worked so hard to perfect! Listen to the tape with your audience, even make notes if you want to, and nod at the most important points. You may feel terribly self-conscious, but the alternative – looking bored, scratching your head – is far worse for your audience.

Presentation software

The PC has become an invaluable presentation tool, used both for preparation and delivery. Later in this chapter we'll look at how PCs can generate spectacular audio-visual presentations, but in this section we'll look at how presentation software can help to produce effective and engaging visual aids.

Software packages designed specifically for presentation preparation make the life of the regular presenter considerably easier, and the end result much more professional. At the time of writing, Microsoft PowerPoint and Lotus Freelance Graphics are among two of the best known and most popular packages, and they have defined a new standard in presentation preparation. The most obvious advantage is the ease with which such software can create professional visuals, by providing the user with a series of templates, saving him or her from the job of complex design and layout. Presenter's notes can also be added to the on-screen version, and printed out for reference.

Using a PC to create your presentation brings a wide range of other advantages, depending upon the software package used:

■ Finished visuals are suitable for reproduction in a variety of formats: printed out onto OHP transparencies; used to generate 35 mm slides or displayed directly onto a screen from the PC (see later in this chapter for more detail).

■ Visuals can be edited or changed at a moment's notice.

■ As finished visuals are stored electronically they can be quickly adapted for other presentations (layout can be changed automatically to fit a different template if necessary).

■ If the PC is to be used to deliver the presentation, then a dazzling array of computer graphics can be used to animate – literally – the visuals you prepare.

■ Digital cameras and video recorders also allow you to incorporate your own photos or film clips into your presentation.

■ Some software packages allow teams to create and edit presentations simultaneously.

■ If preparing coloured visuals, some software allows you to preview your visuals in black and white to assess their value as handout material.

Software designed specifically for presenters can be expensive, and you will need proper training to exploit such software fully. For those who present rarely, or in a less 'hi-tech' context, then a word processing package can produce perfectly acceptable, straightforward text- and image-based visuals. Most good word processors have many of the sophisticated design and layout tools once only available on DTP software. Get to know your word processor better and you may surprise yourself by what you can achieve.

Design and style

Imagine watching a display in which every illustration and visual had been borrowed from other presentations: what impression would you take away with you? Sloppy, scrappy, incoherent, that the presenter didn't really care. In fact, you would remember the complete lack of design and style probably more than you would the main points the presenter was trying to make.

Creating an overall style for your visual material is important, but given the power of computer software, there is no need to hire a professional designer unless you are relying on your presentation to make a significant impact, or to create a highly distinctive 'look'.

Here's how to start a very basic design process. As a first step, let's consider the basic elements of each visual.

VISUAL STYLE

size **and** *style* **of lettering**

where to place text

a logo?

☺ **bullet points or something else?**

colour?

A BORDER - A BORDER - A BORDER - A BORDER - A BORDER - A BORDER?

You need to define the following:

- ■ The size of lettering (the point size) and the different point sizes you want to use for each type of text – main headings, sub-headings, 'body copy' (the main text), captions and so on. Also decide where you want to use capital letters (and more about this on page 121). Make sure your words are, literally, as clear as possible: check that the point size is suitable for the size of venue and audience. Can all the words be read clearly from the back of the room, especially those labelling figures, graphs or pictures? Is the point size too big?
- ■ The style of lettering (the font), and when (or if) you want to use bold, italic or roman script. Most word processing packages offer a wide range of fonts from which to choose so you don't have to stick with just one, but if you decide to mix and match, try to be consistent in their use: one font for all main headings, for example, another for captions and so on. Whatever you choose, make sure each font is easy to read.

■ Where to place text within the frame. No need to be too rigid, but decide a few basic rules and work from there. Is text to be justified or centred, for example? Are points to be made with bullets or simply on separate lines? In practice, you'll find that a variety of layouts adds to the interest of the more basic presentation, but don't choose a wildly different layout for every visual, or the overall impact will be messy and disjointed.

■ Do you want your own logo to appear on each visual? If so, where and how big?

■ If you are using bullet points, do you want to use a simple black dot or something more interesting? Look at the range of symbols available on your word processor.

■ Are you using colour? If so, what colours and when? Remember that you don't always have to use black text on a white background. White text on blue is a popular combination: it's easy to read and the coloured background can help disguise any flaws on your display surface (a marked screen for example). Spot colour – one colour used to highlight certain features (bullet points for example) – can also work well. Avoid using too many bright or garish colours, to help save the eyes of your audience, and remember yellow is a colour to be avoided as it generally doesn't project well.

■ Do you want to frame each visual with a border, or repeat a phrase or logo on each? Marvellous Marketing might add 'Industrial Instruments – Marketing Campaign 1999' along the bottom of each visual. Although this technique personalizes the presentation from the audience's point of view, it will prevent you from using those visuals again, so it's best kept for special occasions.

As you follow these guidelines, you want to achieve a basic level of consistency which gives coherence to the finished presentation. And if you use the same basic guidelines every time, then you'll be able to mix and match from other presentations, saving time and money.

Presenting information visually

Your visual display will underline your spoken presentation, highlighting the key points you wish to make: your visuals must therefore be easy to read and understand, and must not distract from your spoken words.

Aim for clarity and simplicity

Vibrant graphics and innovative design can certainly play a part in the overall package, but use them sparingly – you want your audience to listen to your words and not be actively distracted by the images on the screen. Clear, simple visuals can make just as much impact as the most expensive software-driven display.

The more sophisticated the technology you have at your fingertips, the more tempting it can be to pull out all the stops and create a firework display of colour, motion and sound. But wait. Just imagine the effect of a presentation that never seems to sit still – graphics whizz in and out, images move, colours change – your audience will remember the pyrotechnics but may well forget the message.

And once again, make sure your visuals can be read by all the members of your audience, wherever they are sitting in the room. Double-check that any labels on diagrams or pictures can also be read with ease.

Don't put too much text on each visual

If you do, the audience will stop listening and start reading. If more than four or five points need to be shown together, then stagger their introduction by revealing them one by one. The audience then has a chance to absorb information easily and in a certain order, and you can build your argument in front of them.

Once again, presentation technology can help: double slide projectors or projection software can overlay images, building up to a final, single, visual. A simpler alternative is to create a number of transparencies or slides which gradually increase the number of points to be made: at its most simple, a sheet of opaque paper placed over an OHP transparency can create the same effect, by using it to cover and then reveal, one by one, the points listed. Not so sophisticated, granted, but giving the same end results.

Let's look at some of the visuals Marvellous Marketing are creating. They're working on the section of their presentation where they are talking about themselves. Here's the script:

'Marvellous Marketing was founded in 1975 and has now established a solid reputation for the delivery of cost-effective, successful marketing strategies. In 1990 the agency was awarded the Marketing Association's Osborne Trophy for outstanding achievement – an award which it won again in 1995. Marvellous Marketing is the only regionally based agency to have achieved this double accolade.

'Our client list demonstrates our proven experience in a wide range of industries, and in particular within the scientific and technical sectors, where we can demonstrate specific expertise in the delivery of successful marketing campaigns.'

This information will be used whenever they present, although the emphasis will need to be changed to match each audience. The team already has a 'stock' presentation visual covering their corporate history, which they use for presentations given at short notice, or to more general audiences. Here it is:

- established track record
  - award-winning campaigns
    - wide-ranging industry experience

However, for the presentation to Industrial Instruments, the team takes this basic visual and tailors it more closely to the expectations of the audience:

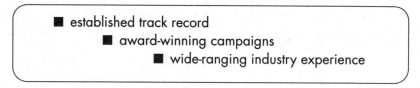

- founded in 1975
- established track record in the scientific and technical sector
- local firm – international expertise
- award-winning marketing campaigns

In fact, editing the longer spoken version produces a far more powerful result, so when preparing your visuals, don't be tempted to put in any more detail than absolutely necessary.

Grammar – ensuring consistency

When your words appear, in letters six inches high, on the screen in front of the audience, it's important that they are absolutely right – and that means spelling and grammar must be spot-on. Word processors may have thesauri, grammar and spell checkers but they cannot be relied upon totally. Misspelling and poor grammar can prove surprisingly irritating to some audiences, and at the very least it indicates a lack of care in your preparation.

So what grammatical points do you need to consider?

- Avoid the random use of capital letters. Because you are writing for a large screen there is a temptation to

    'Write Every Word With A Capital Letter At The Start'

    Don't do it! Capital letters should be reserved for proper names (such as Marvellous Marketing), and other words or phrases which have added significance (for example, the Middle East, Labour, the Bar). If you are using bullet points or lists, decide if you want to start each individual point with a capital letter. You don't have to, but whatever you decide to do, keep the use of capital letters consistent throughout.

- Write dates and times consistently. For example, do you want to write a date as '12 March 1999', 'March 12 1999' or '12/3/99'? Or to use '2.30 pm' or '14.30 hrs'?

- Do the same for numbers over 100 – decide on 15,000 or 15000 or 15k. Don't use roman numerals to number lists.

- If you are going to use company names, make sure they are absolutely correct: check on the use of capital letters, ampersands, and terms such as Inc, Pty, Ltd, Co and plc

- If you use quotations, decide how you want to present them. Here are some of the very many alternatives:

    'Only connect'   "ONLY CONNECT"
    E. M. FORSTER   E M Forster, *Howards End*

    'Only connect'   *'Only connect'*
    E M FORSTER   **E M FORSTER**

- Double-check the spelling and accentuation of any foreign words you might use, especially those which have become anglicized.

■ Avoid full stops in abbreviations (such as BBC, UNESCO, or PhD), or for people's initials (although leave spaces between each letter). As always, there is an exception to the rule: insert a full point after 'no' if you mean 'number', in order to avoid confusion.

■ Treat the following words as singular nouns:
   – company, and all company names, even when they are a theoretical plural. For example: 'Hodder and Stoughton *prints* books'
   – department
   – committee
   – government
   – group
   – majority
   – minority
   – number
   – range
   – staff
   – team
   – 'two-thirds', or any other fraction.

■ Make sure the use of apostrophes is absolutely correct. Never write 'its' when you mean 'it's', 'you're' when you mean 'your' and so on.

■ Make sure commonly confused words are used and spelt correctly. A spelling dictionary will clear up any confusion.

To help you and your colleagues when you check on grammar and spelling, invest in a basic library of reference texts to act as the ultimate arbiter in the arguments that will undoubtedly ensue:

■ A major dictionary to confirm meanings and spellings.

■ A spelling dictionary, to confirm spellings, clarify confusable words, and give a guide to hyphenations and word-breaks.

■ A grammar.

A list of suggested titles can be found at the back of this book.

Another exception. Remember that some of the rules you apply to visual material are design rather than grammatical considerations (for example, dropping full stops at the end of bullet points), so you need not be *too* strict when it comes to applying points of grammar if they impact upon layout – just remember to be consistent.

Check and double-check your final visuals

We've all done it – it's the largest word on the screen, and it's the one which is spelt incorrectly! Proofing your visual material is as important as all the other checks and rehearsals. Ask someone not too closely involved in the presentation to carefully check the text and graphics you've prepared. Your reader should check for spelling errors, consistency in both design and grammatical style, and all the other points covered, using the guidelines in this chapter as a starting point.

Audio-visual equipment – what to use and how to use it

Now let's look in more detail at the best-known presentation equipment, the most appropriate situations in which to use it, pros and cons, and some useful hints and tips.

Presentation equipment is big business, and the pace of change is rapid as manufacturers fight to maintain a technological lead over their rivals. But not all presentations need state-of-the art technology to be successful. The equipment you choose must be appropriate for the type of presentation you plan to give, and this does not always mean the most sophisticated methods you can find. Your final choice will also depend on the resources available to you, but remember you can always borrow or hire more sophisticated equipment if you feel it will make a crucial difference.

Before we start looking at individual options in more detail, let's just look at a few golden rules common to all:

- Never use equipment with which you are unfamiliar: the risk of something going wrong is just too great. This is the reason why low-tech options remain just as popular as ever before, and why audiences continue to accept them without murmur.
- Always stand on the left of the display screen, from the viewpoint of your audience. As they read text, their eyes will be travelling from left to right, so positioning yourself at the left will seem a far more natural place to be, the point at which their eyes automatically return.

■ When presenting, look at the audience, not at the screen, at least not for more than a few moments. It's very tempting to stare at your visuals, along with your audience, but they will still be watching you as you talk, and turning away from them affects the clarity and impact of your delivery.

■ If you need to present in the dark, make sure you know where everything is before you turn the lights off!

Now let's look in detail at the most popular presentation equipment used today, from low- to hi-tech.

Flip chart/whiteboard

The simplest of all presentation media. A flip chart is a very large pad of white paper (lined or unlined) clipped to a lightweight, collapsible easel which can be carried if necessary. Visuals can be either written or drawn on to the flip chart as the presentation progresses, or pre-prepared and uncovered page by page.

A whiteboard is a laminated white surface which can also be magnetic. Whiteboards are usually fixed to the wall, but many flip chart easels also incorporate whiteboards as a backboard to the paper pad. Information is usually written on the whiteboard as the presentation progresses. Magnetic whiteboards can be used to carry other visual items, by the means of small magnetic holders.

What you also need

Flip chart

■ Appropriate marker pens in a range of colours, with back-up supplies (specialized flip chart pens are available from office equipment suppliers, but most marker pens are perfectly adequate, as long as they have a thick enough nib).

■ A pointing device (optional).

Whiteboard

■ Specialized wet or dry marker pens – do *not* use permanent markers! See 'Hints and tips' on when to use what.

■ Whiteboard eraser.

■ A pointing device (optional).

■ Magnetic paper holders.

When to use

If a low-tech option is required (perhaps power is limited or unavailable).

If you need to record audience contributions, especially if you are using another presentation technique at the same time.

If you need to explain points by active illustration.

For less formal, or spontaneous presentations.

When audience numbers are small.

Advantages

Cheap, easy to buy, use and maintain.

Allows for greater spontaneity.

■ The presentation can 'grow' as it is delivered.

No need for a darkened room.

Can be used in conjunction with more 'high-tech' presentation methods.

■ Ideal for any form of audience participation.

Disadvantages

Flip charts

Unless material is pre-prepared, the end result can look scrappy and messy in even the most professional hands.

■ Once written, the running order cannot be changed and in order to return to earlier points you need to flap a lot of paper.

Very neat handwriting is required.

■ Although collapsible easels are promoted as easy to carry, in reality a flip chart still needs a car to be transported effectively and is difficult to keep looking good during transportation.

Only suitable for smaller audiences.

Whiteboards

Again, can look messy and scrappy in use.

■ Size limits the amount of information presented at any one time.

■ Backtracking to earlier information can prove impossible (if it's already been erased).

■ Impossible to transport (unless the easel model is used).

■ Only suitable for smaller audiences.

Hints and tips

■ Unless your handwriting is exceptional, practise writing in capital letters, and at an acceptable speed while retaining legibility. Some flip chart pads are lined with faint rules or grids: these can help if you need to draw diagrams.

■ Practise writing from the side, so as not to obscure the board. If you're one of a team who will all be writing, make sure both left- and right-handed individuals have enough room in which to operate.

■ Make sure you have plenty of spare pens and erasers.

■ Make sure your flip chart has enough pages for your whole presentation.

■ If your presentation is pre-prepared, number or code page corners so that you can access specific pages quickly.

■ If you can't pre-draw figures or diagrams, devise extremely simple versions which you can execute quickly.

■ Make sure an earlier presentation, or other material, isn't lurking in the middle of the flip chart.

■ When using a whiteboard, choose 'dry erase' pens if you plan to change or alter information during the presentation, and need to erase it quickly. 'Wet erase' pens provide a more permanent finish which will not smudge so easily when the board is in use (although marks are still easy to remove with an eraser).

■ Don't use yellow pens – your audience won't be able to read the words.

Portfolio

A hard backed folder of any size, usually zipped, with clear document pockets or prepared boards inside, either bound into the folder or held in place as in a ring binder. A rigid fold-out section (an extension of one of the covers) provides a support, enabling the portfolio to stand alone on a tabletop. Presentation material is flipped over page by page.

When to use

- Presentations to a small audience (no more than four or five).
- Presentations which are frequently repeated.
- Presentations which need to be delivered quickly, in any venue – from a boardroom to a car park.

Advantages

- Very easy to use: lightweight, takes only seconds to put up.
- Cheap and easy to buy.
- Ideal for set presentations which are used again and again.
- Can easily be stored in a car boot, and carried like a briefcase.
- Running order can be changed quickly and easily.
- Needs no power or special facilities – a presentation can be given in virtually any circumstances.
- Results can be very professional.

Disadvantages

- Suitable only for a very small audience.
- Content is limited by the capacity of the portfolio.

Hints and tips

- When choosing a portfolio, ensure it is robust, gives good protection when in transit and can be put into the upright position with ease. Also check that the portfolio takes clear wallets of a standard, easily obtainable design.
- If using the same portfolio presentation regularly check the contents thoroughly each time you use it (to make sure nothing has been 'borrowed' by colleagues). Update information frequently so that the portfolio is ready for use at a moment's notice.
- As you will probably be presenting to a very small group notes, cards and other *aides-mémoires* can look ridiculous. Make sure you can deliver your presentation by using the visuals as your only prompt.
- When setting up, beware of reflections on the clear surface of the portfolio's pockets, especially if highly reflective plastic has been used. Ensure your audience is not affected by any glare before you start.

Overhead projector (OHP)

An OHP comprises a light source with a clear plate above or below it. Visuals are prepared on transparent media (traditionally acetate sheets), and are placed on the clear plate. The light illuminates the transparency, which is then reflected, magnified and projected by an angled mirror and lens held above it onto a flat screen positioned in front of the audience. OHPs can also be used in conjunction with a Liquid Crystal Display (LCD) projection panel or tablet. This panel is linked directly to the PC, and acts as a transparent PC screen, using the OHP to project the PC screen display onto the larger flat screen. LCD panels are examined in more detail on page 134.

Most people are familiar with large, bulky OHP equipment, but much slimmer models are also available, designed to collapse into a briefcase sized box for easy transportation. Newer models are brighter, reducing the need for complete darkness, and they will illuminate an image more evenly across the screen. Some models offer colour tuning, auto-sheet feeders, and flip in magnifiers for close detail.

What you also need

- A power supply and possibly an extension lead, to give more flexibility when positioning your equipment. Use parcel tape to secure any loose cable to the floor (but make sure it's not too adhesive or you'll have trouble removing it quickly when you need to pack up and go).
- A screen or pale coloured blank wall on which to project the image.
- A table on which to position the OHP. It should be large enough for both the equipment and your transparencies or computer.
- Spare bulb(s) for the OHP lightbox (and a handkerchief with which to hold the hot bulb if you are called upon to change it mid-presentation).
- Pointing device (optional).
- An opaque piece of paper (if you need to cover part of a transparency).
- Special marker pens (if you plan to write on or annotate acetate transparencies).
- A soft cloth to polish the lens and mirror.

When to use

The ubiquity of the OHP is one reason why it remains among the most popular of all presentation technologies, despite the growing availability of far more sophisticated alternatives. An OHP is acceptable in almost any presentation situation, from the largest auditorium to a one-to-one meeting, and is also useful as a back-up for more complex multi-media presentations.

Advantages

Easy to use – most people can become proficient with only a little practice.

Easy to find – most offices, hotels and other business venues have an OHP. All you need to take with you are your transparencies (as long as the venue has spare bulbs, marker pens and so on).

Reliable – common faults can be easily rectified, even mid-way through a presentation.

Basic models are cheap to buy or rent.

Portable models are available.

Can be used for both small and large audiences.

Allows the re-ordering of visuals at the last minute.

Allows the presenter to annotate visuals as the presentation progresses. Some OHPs incorporate rolls of blank acetate film which can be used in the same way as a flip chart or whiteboard, by scrolling through as the presentation progresses.

Newer OHPs are sufficiently bright to provide a good image even in a well-lit venue.

Disadvantages

Can appear 'old-fashioned', especially if the equipment you are using is old.

Older equipment can also be quite noisy, creating an ugly physical presence within the presentation venue.

Older equipment will need a dimmed room in which to be operated.

Transparencies need protection when in transit.

- Needs a power supply and a space large enough for the screen and the projected image.
- Can be noisy and distracting, especially in a smaller group.
- Poor at reproducing photos or finely detailed graphics. Colours can also fade when projected.

Hints and tips

Note: For hints and tips on using LCD screens and OHPs see pages 136–7.

- Different OHPs project onto different maximum screen sizes, so if presenting to a large audience, make sure the OHP you plan to use will project an image of sufficient size for all the audience to see.
- When setting up the OHP, make sure you have enough table space either side on which to place both the transparencies you are to use, and those you have just shown.
- Check that larger OHPs don't obscure the view for some members of the audience. If so, try a lower table, or arrange audience seating well to the side of the projection equipment. Likewise, make sure you stand in such a way as not to cast a shadow on the screen whilst presenting.
- Lightly polish the mirror and lens before starting, and check the lightbox for any blemishes that might be projected up onto the screen, affecting the clarity of your image. A soft cloth may help remove them.
- If the projected image is distorted when on the screen, raise the back legs of the OHP to return the image to a perfect square.
- Turning the OHP on and off repeatedly can stress the bulb. Try to structure your presentation to avoid this happening.
- An introductory transparency, perhaps simply the title of your presentation or your company logo, can prove very useful. You can use it as a 'test' transparency, especially if you have to set up while your audience is entering the room, or it can be placed on the OHP and left there while your audience seats itself. This removes the need to start up the OHP as the first action of your presentation.

- Practise changing transparencies until the movement is seamless and fluid. A blank screen should be visible only for the shortest period of time.
- Consider mounting transparencies in cardboard frames. They provide a useful handling device, and can be numbered for ease of reference. You can even write notes on the mount itself. The only disadvantage is that they make each transparency bigger, so check that your briefcase or document wallet is large enough to protect them properly, if you have to transport them any distance.
- Place a blank sheet of paper between each transparency. This makes the acetates easier to see and handle.
- Acetate can be heat sensitive, and so needs careful handling when in use and subsequently in storage. Don't leave acetates on an illuminated projector for any length of time.

35 mm slide projector

The slide projector is another familiar presentation method, long used in both business and in the home. In essence, transparent slides are placed in front of a light source which then projects the image, through a magnifying lens, onto a screen or blank wall. This technology has become increasingly sophisticated over the years: remote control projectors are now the norm; visuals can be synchronized with a prepared soundtrack; multiple lenses can blend one slide into the next without a blank screen intervening. Further design improvements have increased brightness, so that they need not be used in the dark, and brighter light sources have increased the 'throw' of the beam, improving reproduction in bigger venues. Improved heat dissipation technology has helped avoid hot spots, resulting in better colour reproduction.

What you also need

- Power supply and extension lead.
- Table for the projector (which can be raised above the head height of the seated audience, if possible).
- Separate table or lectern for the presenter (especially if the projector is operated by remote control).

■ Specialized pointing device such as a laser pointer or specialized torch (optional – see page 137 for more on laser pointers).

When to use

■ Suitable for any occasion, and any audience size, although you will need to make sure that the projected image is large enough for the size of venue.

■ Ideal for presentations in which clear visuals are vital: slide reproductions of photos, graphics, coloured images and so on will all appear with pinpoint accuracy.

Advantages

■ Tried and trusted technology, easy to buy or hire.

■ Delivers a colourful, professional presentation.

■ Images are clear and crisp, and colour can be used to great effect.

■ Remote control gives 'hands-free' operation, allowing the presenter to concentrate on the presentation.

■ Easy to carry and set up, and straightforward to operate.

■ Slides are easy to store and index, and are robust in transit.

Disadvantages

■ Can place a 'barrier' between the presenter and his or her audience, more so than the OHP (which does allow more direct interaction, especially if the presenter is adding comments directly to the visuals as they are displayed).

■ Needs power source and usually a darkened room (although some projectors are now bright enough to operate effectively in daylight).

■ Can be inflexible once in operation (unless the slide show is being generated directly from the PC).

■ Slide production is relatively expensive, especially if the slides will only be used once.

■ Unless you have facilities in house, slides have to be produced by a specialist agency and time must be allowed for design and delivery. Last-minute changes can be difficult to accommodate.

■ Slide projectors are not quite as common as OHPs and so unless you have your own, you will have to rent or borrow and transport the equipment to the venue. Slide equipment is not as robust as OHPs – if you're using borrowed or shared equipment it needs to be double-checked before use.

Hints and tips

Note: Refer to hints and tips about using OHPs for information on screens and projecting in general.

■ If you are presenting in a darkened room, make sure you have enough light to see your notes. A lectern with an in-built lamp is useful in this context, otherwise prepare to speak without notes.

■ Double-check the order of slides once installed by running them quickly through the projector before your audience arrives. Mark the top right-hand corner of each slide to provide a quick visual check that no slides are upside down.

■ Keep a hard copy of the information to hand, especially to check running order.

■ For an easy to index and quick to view archive, scan frequently used slides onto a CD-ROM: these can then be viewed via a PC.

PC/Multimedia presentation technology

There are many different ways of exploiting the power of the PC in a presentation. Increasingly sophisticated software packages enable the presenter to deliver a vibrant mix of graphics, moving and still images, photos, video clips, sound and music. The general term for this technology is 'multimedia' – technology capable of exploiting information in both video and data format.

If the PC incorporates a modem, then it can also download images, pages or whole presentations from other PCs or on-line sources (Internet or Intranet).

When seen in demonstration, PC-generated presentations can be very impressive indeed, but before you throw away your OHP, it's important to understand fully the implications of using such technology. An important issue is the power of the hardware you have at your disposal, in terms of processing capability and memory: a PC can generate a stunning presentation, but if it can't deliver the images you've created at an acceptable speed, then your presentation will become an embarrassment. Consult a computer specialist before investing in any new equipment, or sophisticated software, to make sure you have all the power you need to use it properly. And as you can probably guess from that last statement, you may need to spend a considerable sum if you want to use the most sophisticated software tools available. You will have to judge whether it is worth making the investment, basing your decision on the frequency with which you present, and the relative sophistication of the audiences you usually talk to.

As in all other areas of computing, technological development is fast and furious. At the time of writing, the following have become established presentation options:

- LCD (Liquid Crystal Display) tablets or projection panels – flat transparent panels linked to a computer, which act as a PC screen. The tablet sits on an OHP which projects the PC-generated presentation onto a larger screen or wall. Sound can be delivered via the PC itself, using multi-media speakers.

- LCD and DLP (Digital Light Processing) projectors – taking the slide projector one step further, these projectors can transmit PC generated presentations onto a screen, and deliver stereo sound. Certain models also offer remote controls which can act as a computer 'mouse', controlling the PC from the display screen. Projectors produce a brighter image than a tablet or panel, and range from 'ultra-portable' (designed for use with a laptop PC for the ultimate in travelling presentations) to fixed models, designed for use in conference halls or training facilities: varying performance levels give associated levels of brightness and resolution (with an associated increase in cost).

- Large-screen PCs – laptop or desktop. These act in the same way as portfolios, and are suitable when presenting to a small group of four or five. Small multimedia speakers can be used to supply sound if necessary. The rapid development in the power of notebook and laptop computers have allowed travelling presenters to exploit the power of PC-generated presentations. The most expensive models incorporate larger brighter screens, CD-ROM facilities and can handle complex graphics at an acceptable speed. Less expensive models don't have the power to deliver the most sophisticated presentations, but will still provide a highly professional result.

When to use

If a state-of-the-art presentation is called for (perhaps you are an organization selling high-tech products) then such technology is the only answer. It is also ideal when a more complex mix of graphics, pictures and possibly video is called for, especially if you want to manipulate your images while presenting, for example, to show the effect of different results on a set of statistics. Given the sophistication of available technology, it is particularly appropriate for competitive situations, or in those situations when you need to make a very good impression. But it's also very useful for presentations which are given frequently, or which may change at very short notice.

Advantages

- Has the potential to deliver a very impressive, memorable presentation.
- Very flexible and can be changed at very short notice. For example, if you are giving the same presentation twice in one day, details can be changed or improvements made between presentations simply by editing the files on your PC. This can represent significant savings in costs, especially compared to slide production, and allows you to respond immediately to audience feedback.
- If the projection equipment is available at the venue, a laptop computer may be the only equipment you need to take with you.
- LCD/DLP projectors can almost always be used in a normally lit room.

Disadvantages

- There is a much higher risk of something going wrong during the presentation – you'll need to arm yourself with both presentation and computing expertise in order to be fully prepared.

■ Compatibility between your PC and the projection equipment cannot always be guaranteed, especially if the latter is not your own.

■ Ironically, the more options you have at your fingertips, the more the temptation to overuse them. The result can appear over the top and distracting.

■ If using just a computer screen, impact will necessarily be limited by screen size.

■ High-technology aids are expensive and even though prices fall year on year, they are still by far the most expensive option available.

■ The more complex the equipment, the more difficult to use: more training and practice is required in order to present effectively.

■ The brighter the image, the more heat is produced. This will be dissipated either by fans (which can be noisy) or vents, which can prove distracting, especially if the unit is placed among your audience (on a boardroom table, for example).

■ If using a tablet or projector, the resulting image will still not be as crisp as that produced by slides, and this may be crucial if detail is important.

Hints and tips

Note: Refer to hints and tips about using OHPs for information on screens and projecting in general.

■ Practise, practise, practise! A specialized training course is a wise investment if you plan to use such equipment regularly, and a thorough knowledge of the ins and outs of the PC and the software you will be using is essential.

■ Practise setting up your equipment with equal intensity, especially if you are the only one presenting. You need to understand both your hardware and software in order to deal with any unexpected developments (and remember the risk of this happening is much greater). If you are part of a team, make sure you are not the only one who understands how the whole thing works.

- Given the greater risk of things going badly wrong, back up your presentation onto two sets of disks, and bring a full contingency presentation if at all possible. An OHP and a set of transparencies summarizing your presentation will prove a lifesaver if your PC decides to stop working at a crucial moment. A knowledgeable colleague who can act as 'technician' during your presentation is also a useful help.

- Make sure that the PC or laptop you plan to use has sufficient power to deliver the presentation at an acceptable speed, especially if you want to show complex graphics, video clips or frequently changing images.

- If you plan to make an external link during your presentation – to another PC or to the Internet, for example – make sure you have a back-up version of what you intended to show on disk, in case technology lets you down.

- LCD panels require OHPs with light boxes placed below the transparent image – some OHPs (particularly some portable models) place the light source above the transparency.

- A presentation can be networked across a number of PCs, or delivered via CD-ROM – see page 138 for more information.

Laser pointers

The laser pointer, a hand-held pen-shaped device which shines a laser beam onto the display surface, has come in for much bad press of late. The sharp-focus beam such pointers produce can reach distances of up to 75 m, and can dazzle or even damage the eyes of anyone inadvertently crossing the beam's path.

Many audience members find them actively annoying, and a distraction when in use. A traditional telescopic pointer can serve the same function equally as well, unless you are presenting next to a giant screen. If you do need to use a laser pointer, turn it on and off whilst pointing at the screen. If left shining, the natural impulse to wave your hands around will send your audience diving under their seats.

CD, Internet and video presentations

Although strictly beyond the remit of this chapter, CD, Internet and video presentations are worth mentioning. If you need to present to a large number of people spread over a wide area, or need to deliver the same material a number of times, then they may be a practical alternative to spending weeks of your time travelling up and down the country, delivering the same presentation time and time again. You can deliver your presentation much as you would in a boardroom or conference venue, illustrate your talk with visual aids, but rather than invite your audience to a given venue, let them watch it at their convenience.

In particular, pre-recorded Internet and CD presentations bring an added range of benefits. A much greater range of information can be built into the presentation, most of it accessible by choice (by selecting and clicking on an on-screen icon). Viewers can have the option of viewing a whole presentation or individual segments, and the whole event can be replayed as often as necessary, and circulated among colleagues.

'Live' Internet presentations also allow 'real time' interaction, using 'digital whiteboards' and 'raised electronic hands'. Once again, the power and impact of both Internet and CD rely on the viewer using a sufficiently powerful PC. And even then, Internet presentations can still be very slow, especially if complex graphics or video clips need to be downloaded. The development of improved Internet links, capable of carrying much larger quantities of information, will solve this problem in the future.

Also in the future, but not too distant, is the wider availability of DVD (digital video or versatile disc) technology. DVDs can hold much greater quantities of information than CDs, with better 'playback' quality than both CD or VHS. They may offer even greater potential for pre-recorded presentations.

Creating such a presentation often requires a specialist team to help script, design, film or press, edit and produce the finished article, especially the video version and a number of such organizations can be found in the trade telephone directory. They can also find professional actors to 'give' your presentation, if you feel you would perform badly in this context. Extracts from such videos, perhaps specific speeches from certain individuals, can also be used again, as part of a multi-media presentation.

Practice and training

Once you have decided upon a specific technique, make sure you build sufficient time into your planning schedule for dedicated practice, and always use the presentation technology you have selected in your dress rehearsals.

If you are using someone else's equipment then it's important to ensure you have time – even if it's only five or ten minutes – to become familiar with it before you use it, no matter how well practised you are with the technique involved.

As presentation techniques become more sophisticated, then you may want to 'upgrade' your skills to keep up with the competition, or to test your skills before you need to give a real presentation. If this is the case, then formal training is probably the answer. Any number of organizations can provide training in presentation techniques, and local business training advice centres can provide contact details.

Summary

Structure your visual aids to underline the main points of your presentation, using text, illustration, video or audio.

Presentation software makes the creation of visuals considerably easier, and gives a very professional result.

Aim to create a consistent overall 'look' when developing your visuals, but be creative within these parameters.

Clarity is vital.

Double-check grammar and spelling.

Only use audio-visual equipment with which you are comfortable – otherwise get training before you use it professionally.

The more technically sophisticated the technique you choose, the greater the chance of things going wrong.

Do it yourself

■ Look at the section on pages 128–31, covering the use of OHPs. Treat this as a presentation script, and draft four text-based visuals which could accompany your spoken words. Once you're happy with the text, create a basic design outline. Summarize:

- equipment and accessories
- advantages
- disadvantages
- hints and tips.

■ What audio-visual aids (if any) are suitable for the following scenarios:

- a speech to shareholders, given in a theatre
- the presentation of 'thoughts' to two colleagues
- a competitive business pitch, in the computer industry
- a credentials presentation, given in an office reception area.

■ Marvellous Marketing is using an OHP, Tom Collins a PC – what could Sarah Williams and Bill Bailey employ?

6 ARRIVALS, DEPARTURES AND IN BETWEEN: PRESENTATION ETIQUETTE

It's easy to focus entirely on delivering your presentation, and forget that you may well be 'on show' from the moment you arrive at the presentation venue to when you leave. It's important to remember these opening and closing stages, and prepare for them as much as possible. Most of the advice given in this section refers to the larger, more formal presentation but even the simplest portfolio presentation will benefit from a little forethought about what to do when you arrive and set up. Simply adapt the advice below to suit your own circumstances.

Setting up and settling in

It's important, especially when presenting away from home, to allow yourself as much time as possible to arrive and 'settle in'. Build this time into your overall presentation planning schedule: this is the time when you can make sure everything is perfect, and also steady your nerves and relax.

If you are presenting within your own building, then this phase should be relatively straightforward: simply make sure that the room you are using is booked for an hour or so before the start of the presentation. If you are presenting first thing in the morning, then book the room from the evening before, and complete your basic setting up then. This greatly reduces stress levels on the morning of the presentation, and buys you some useful time if you are late arriving (which of course you won't be!). Put up a sign on the door of the room to tell others that the set-up inside is not to be moved or disturbed.

If you are presenting away from home, then setting-up time often becomes far more of a luxury. If you are presenting alone, then arrange your setting-up time well in advance: make sure you have enough time to go through the checklist detailed below, but don't exploit your host's good nature too much. Depending upon the complexity of the presentation you plan to give, make sure you can complete your preparations in around 15 to 20 minutes. If you are presenting at an independent venue, then you will have to discuss such arrangements with the venue manager and see how much time you will be allowed.

In some presentation situations, you will find yourself in a 'queue' of other organizations, all timetabled to present during the same day. Time will therefore be more limited and much more strictly controlled. You will have to assess whether you can set up the sort of presentation you want to give in the time allowed, or whether you need to downscale your plans, or increase your team of assistants.

If at all possible, don't set up while the audience watches you, for a host of obvious reasons: you won't be relaxed; you may want to preview visuals that you don't want your audience to see; you won't look your best with your jacket off, on your hands and knees, taping electrical cable to the floor.

Ideally, you or your team will set up and then invite your audience in, but sometimes this may not be possible, especially if you are ushered into a room where the audience is waiting. In such a situation, the audience may suggest a break for five or ten minutes – if they don't, then very politely suggest it yourself. But if you can, run through as many checks as possible outside the presentation room.

Setting up checklist

Whatever the context, run through the following every time you set up:

Seating and tabling arrangements

Are there enough chairs for your audience, your presentation team (if you have one), your assistants and, of course, yourself? Make sure a few spares are easily available for unexpected arrivals and leave them either at the back of the presentation room, or just outside the door (you may need to add a notice asking people not to remove them). Make sure there are enough tables for your presentation equipment: look back at Chapter 5 to double-check on the type of furniture you will need.

Set up and check any presentation equipment

When presenting away from home, or using borrowed equipment, you will need to double-check that everything works as you expect it to. Test the power supply, make sure screens are clean, flip charts are empty all the way through, pens are in place, spare bulbs are easily accessible and so on, depending upon the technique you plan to use. Check there are no trailing leads which might trip you or your colleagues up as you cross the stage. If it looks like this might be the case, tape the wires to the floor with parcel tape.

Run through the order of any visuals

A final check not only reassures you that everything is in its rightful place, but also provides a final reminder of your forthcoming presentation, helping to steady the nerves. Remember to prepare an introductory visual to use when testing equipment, and to show on the screen before and after the presentation.

Set out presentation materials and displays

Any notes, handouts, pens, pointers, props, drinking water and so on should all be in place before the audience sits down. You may also be mounting a display in the presentation room: if so, allow sufficient time to set this up to the standard you require, but make sure you can achieve this in the time you have available.

Check on any arrangements for entertaining

Depending on what you have planned, make sure the caterers have arrived and are happy, that the coffee has started to brew, and that enough clean cups and saucers (and spoons) are ready. Tell your caterers when you expect to break for refreshments, so that they can be prepared.

'Dress the set'

As noted in Chapter 2, when we looked at how to assess a venue, it's easy to improve the overall appearance of a room and make it look smarter and more welcoming. A plain cloth can instantly smarten the most battered office table, as can a vase of fresh flowers. A strategically placed floor plant, borrowed from elsewhere in the building, can hide a multitude of dirty marks and stained carpet tiles, and also soften an otherwise bleak room. Don't overdo it, but consider how you could make the room a little more attractive and inviting, positively contributing to a more relaxed atmosphere and a professional presentation.

Start a 'presentation box'

Your 'presentation box' will be your best friend on the big day. Keep it, untouched, in a corner of the office, and fill it with all the things that come in useful when setting up: scissors, sticky tape, parcel tape, sticky pads or adhesive putty, a screwdriver, string, a stapler, spare card and marker pens, fuses, light bulbs, dusters, a tablecloth and so on. With each presentation you will find some new indispensable item to add.

'Before we begin . . .'

We've already looked at how to start 'with a bang', but before you launch into the presentation proper, make sure you've introduced yourself.

When to introduce yourself depends greatly upon the circumstances of the presentation you are giving, but the most important thing is to remember to do it, especially if you are presenting as a team. You may find this happens in a reception area, but, depending once again upon your circumstances and judgement, formally introducing your presentation team makes a good prelude to the presentation proper.

When introducing yourself and your colleagues, include the following:

- name
- job title
- the reason they are presenting.

Once the presentation is underway, reiterating this information may be useful as part of initial handovers. If you are part of a panel presentation, then you may be required to introduce yourself, so make sure you have a brief résumé prepared, one that highlights the reasons why you have been asked to join the presentation panel.

Once the presenters have been introduced, then it might be worthwhile to outline briefly how the presentation will be structured, so the audience knows what to expect.

If your presentation is to take half a day or more (a training presentation for example), then quickly talk your audience through the timetable you've prepared, highlighting breaks for refreshments, and touching on practical details such as directions to toilets, nearby telephones and so on.

Obviously, if you are presenting at the request of your audience, then such details are irrelevant, but at the very least let your audience know how you want to manage questions and answers, so they know they can interrupt with impunity, or that they should take notes and save their questions for the end of the presentation.

Planning introductions

Let's see how our presenters are planning to introduce themselves and their presentations. Marvellous Marketing are delivering a formal presentation which has already prompted a meeting between some of the individuals concerned – they'll have to acknowledge this in their introduction, which is being given by Pauline Palmer, the managing director of the company. This is what she has sketched out as a suitable introduction:

'Good morning, my name is Pauline Palmer and I'm the managing director of Marvellous Marketing. I'd like to start by thanking you for inviting us to present to you today and before we begin, I'd like to introduce the other members of our team, whom I know some of you have met already. With me I have Fergus Davis, consultant and export specialist, and Jane Smith, consultant, who would act as account director if we were to work for Industrial Instruments.

'In our presentation we will address the issues you have raised with us by outlining a strategic marketing campaign which will deliver the results your company needs: we'll also demonstrate our experience and ability in this particular field, experience which will prove vital in maintaining the campaign's success. I'm sure our presentation will generate many questions, and if possible, we would like to take these at the end of the presentation.

'So, I'd like to formally begin by handing over to Jane . . .'

Tom Collins is presenting in a less formal context, but one in which his audience is no less interested in what he has to say, and how he's going to say it. Tom wants them to know straight away how he's going to structure the presentation, so the audience knows what to expect:

'Good evening everybody, and thank you for coming along this evening. My name is Tom Collins, and I run a small company, based here in Old Town, called Information for Business. I'm here tonight to reveal the secrets of the Internet, and how it can help you in your working life, but before I begin, can I draw your attention to the timetable, which is in the wallet in front of you. As you can see, I've divided the presentation into two distinct sections, and I hope I've allowed plenty of time for questions and answers, but please feel free to ask me anything at any time as it's important you all understand the points being made as we move through the presentation.

'So, to begin . . .'

Remembering names and faces – for you and your audience

Faced with a small sea of unfamiliar faces, it can be hard enough to remember your presentation, let alone new names and job titles. Some of us are always bad at remembering names and although we know we don't do it on purpose, it can appear rude. Likewise, an audience may find it difficult to remember your name and those of your presentation team, especially if you are one of a series of presentations given that day.

It's rare that you have to remember the name of everyone in the room, but if it's important that you do then the following suggestions may help:

- Find out exactly who you will be presenting to: their names, job titles, influence, relevance to the outcome of the presentation and so on. If the audience is small enough, memorize the names of all those attending, especially those you have never met before. If you are already familiar with their names when you meet them, then it will simply be a matter of putting faces to those names. Keep your list of audience names with you in your presentation notes – it will be a useful memory jogger.

- If remembering names is a constant problem, look into some memory tricks which might suit you: however, remembering the mnemonic might be just as much a problem! Alternatively, practise out of context, when you're not so stressed: cut out some pictures of people, take some random names, and try to remember them all using whatever method seems to work. Once your technique is honed, try to use it whenever you can (watching TV game shows, for example, try to remember the names of all the contestants) so that you can maintain your skill.

- If you are presenting as a team, help your audience by preparing a page of 'potted biographies' of yourself and your colleagues to hand out before you start to present.

- If you are presenting as a panel, perhaps contributing to a core subject, then name plates could be used, made from word processed sheets mounted on card. Make sure they can be read from the back row of the audience, if possible (although don't make them so large as to look obtrusive or ridiculous). Such name plates come in very useful during question and answer sessions, when the audience can address questions directly at the most relevant speaker.

- When presenting to a small group whose names you don't know, invite each member to identify themselves and give their job titles. Obviously, you must judge just how appropriate this request will be: board directors may not take too kindly to being treated as trainees, but this technique does work well in more 'neutral' situations such as training presentations, or informative presentations. Have a piece of paper and pen to hand and map out the position of each audience member to remind you of who is sitting where.

- Another option is to invite the audience to write their own names on a piece of paper and then to place this in front of them (assuming they are all seated at tables), or on lapel badges (try to find a badge suitable for wearing on dresses and plain tops as most are designed to clip on to the breast pocket of a suit jacket). Remember that you will be unable to read lapel badges easily when you stand to present, but that they are useful if you want audience members to interact with each other, in games or other exercises.

Forgetting a name

If the worst comes to the worst, and you simply cannot remember a name, you can try to get around the problem. The best tactic is simply to apologize: 'I'm dreadfully sorry, I didn't quite catch your name' might work. However, it might be better to be honest and say 'I'm awfully sorry, I've got an appalling memory for names, you'll have to forgive my rudeness if I ask you for your name again'. You can also use such phrases as 'your colleague' to refer to someone whose name has temporarily escaped you (although obviously this will only work when the conversation is between more than two people).

When to use handout materials

One of the most commonly questioned points of presentation etiquette. Is it better to hand out accompanying material before, after or during the presentation? In practice, every presentation places different demands upon its audience, so the only way to decide how to manage the handouts you prepare is to weigh up the following considerations:

Does the audience need to know any information before the presentation begins?

If you are planning a presentation which is divided into clear stages, then a timetable or running order should be given out as soon as the audience arrives. Biographical background to the presenter or team is also better handed out up front, or sent on ahead if your presentation is a more formal affair. Such information can be given to your audience as it arrives, or left on seats for delegates to pick up as they sit down. If you are presenting formally to a small group of people, then personally handing material out might be the more practical option.

Do you want to have the audience's unwavering attention?

If your presentation relies on an element of surprise, or on the logical unfolding of an argument, then you run the risk of ruining everything if you hand out material too soon and you'll find that some members of your audience will spend their time flicking through the material you have provided, rather than concentrating on the presentation. So don't hand out anything that reveals what you are about to say: assure your audience that relevant material, covering all the main points, will be handed out after the presentation, so they don't feel they have to scribble everything down.

If your presentation is delivered in stages, then stagger your handouts to match and print each set on different coloured paper, to make them easier to sort and identify.

Will your audience need to take notes?

In some presentations, instructive and informative especially, most audience members may feel a little unhappy listening to the speaker without making notes. But you the presenter may feel unhappy talking to an audience constantly scribbling, and never looking up. If this is the case, assure your audience from the outset that full handouts will be available covering all the points made – and make sure your handout material delivers exactly that.

If you're happy that your audience takes brief notes, then a compromise would be to hand out hard copies of your visual aids and invite your audience to annotate those.

Will your audience leave immediately after the presentation, or will they stay on?

If you are planning to offer your audience refreshments after your presentation, or give them an opportunity to look at displays, demonstrations or to talk to the presentation team, then they might find it impractical to keep hold of any information you have given them, especially if they are also holding finger food and cups or glasses. Many sets of handouts will be left, abandoned, in corners of the room or on seats. The best solution is to create additional, full sets of handouts and have them available for delegates to take as they depart, perhaps by setting up a small table by the door. This will ensure that everyone receives the information they require. If they don't want to take it with them, offer to post or deliver the material to their offices as soon as possible. Another possibility is to personalize each set of handouts with each delegate's name (assuming you know all the names in advance). Lost or missing sets of material can then easily be forwarded to their rightful owners.

Handout strategies in action

What handout materials are our presentation teams planning to put together, and how have they decided to use them?

For Marvellous Marketing, their presentation focuses on the proposal document which represents the main handout, and will be given to the audience as it departs. However, they do want to prepare additional material. This is their strategy:

1 **Send out in advance** to each member of the audience:
   - potted biographies of each team member
   - company brochure
   - covering letter.

2 **Hand out after the presentation:**
   - proposal document (with supportive material included as appendices)
   - bound copies of visuals.

For Tom Collins's audience, the handouts will play an important role in helping them remember what they have learnt. His plan covers a number of different strategies:

1 **Post on in advance**: summary of talk/details of what to bring/background reading/questionnaire on levels of knowledge.

2 **Put on seats** before audience arrives: timetable of talk/ information on me and the company.

3 **Notes on presentation**: instructions/activities/workshops: divide between stages – hand out at start of each stage.

4 **To take with them as they leave**: copies of most important visuals/sources of further info/reading list/company brochure and contact details.

Ending a presentation and leaving the venue

Most presentations will close with a question and answer session, or some form of audience feedback, and so, in effect, your presentation will have two endings: the 'big bang' ending, and the close of the question and answer session which must be just as carefully managed.

If you have been invited to present, then the audience, or audience 'leader', will keep a close eye on the clock and should close the presentation for you by concluding any questioning. When this point has been reached, take the opportunity to thank your hosts for asking you to present, and invite them to follow up with any further questions by phone or by a further meeting.

If you are controlling the presentation, then set a time limit for questions and answers and if it proves too generous, then rather than face a dispiriting silence simply curtail the session and conclude the presentation, thanking the audience for attending, and inviting them to see you separately if they would like further information.

When the presentation is finally complete, pack up as quickly and as efficiently as you can – replace your belongings neatly in the boxes in which they were stored rather than grabbing bundles of papers and running for a reception area in which to sort them out. Double-check that you have left nothing behind, especially if you are using borrowed presentation equipment. Are your slides still in the presenter? Is the last transparency still on the OHP? If you've been using a whiteboard, make sure it's clean and ready for the next user. If you are presenting as a team, then allot each member specific responsibilities which will make the whole task even simpler.

Make sure you have thanked the person who has asked you to present (or it may be the case that they are thanking you) and leave.

Summary

- Make sure you allow enough time to set up and check the venue and equipment properly.
- Start to put together a presentation box which holds all the useful bits and pieces you might need.
- Make sure you and your team have been properly introduced before you begin.
- Pack up quickly and don't leave anything behind.

Do it yourself

- Write a list of items to put in your own presentation box and then gather them all together.
- Draft a friendly, relatively informal introduction for Bill Bailey's presentation to the new recruits at Crazy Crackers Ltd. What should Bill and Sarah's strategy for handout material be? Remember, the recruits will be given refreshments and then will go off around the building. What's the best way to make sure they won't lose any handouts they may be given?

7 | POST-PRESENTATION ANALYSIS

The presentation has been delivered, all went well and you can breathe a sigh of relief: but you're probably thinking that it could have gone better, that a certain detail was overlooked, and that a bit more practice would have improved things no end. How do you manage the post-presentation phase effectively, so that you can make the most of, and build upon, your most recent experience? And how can you make sure that your audience's expectations were met?

To manage the post-presentation stage effectively, you'll need to look at every aspect and analyze what did and didn't work and feed this experience back into your next presentation – and that of your colleagues. This last point is quite important: if you don't present very often, then pooled experience can prove an invaluable source of information and will highlight both good and bad practice.

Planning the post-presentation phase

Start by examining all the different aspects that you want to assess: it might be worthwhile constructing a brief form, for internal use, on which you could note down any information in a logical format. You'll want to look at:

- what went well
- what went badly
- things that didn't happen quite as expected and what you did in response (it's always useful to know what other people did in a crisis)
- other thoughts that occurred as the presentation was underway.

See the following for examples.

Strategy

Did the final presentation match the brief you were given? Did you predict the expectations of your audience correctly? Was the style and tone of your presentation appropriate? If there were any hidden agendas, did you cope with them successfully?

Planning and preparation

Did your planning stay on schedule? Were all practical arrangements made successfully? Did you find any useful new suppliers of equipment or good venues that should be added to a central database? Were rehearsals effective practice for the real event?

Content

Did you make an effective beginning? Did your presentation address all the points that were outlined in your brief? Were all your main points clearly made and in a relevant order? Did the audience get involved as you had expected? Was your conclusion effective and well received? Were your *aides-mémoires* a help or a hindrance? Were your handouts well received? How did the question and answer session go? Were any questions completely unexpected? What did this part of the presentation tell you about your audience's reception of what went before?

Visual aids

Did you make the right choice of presentation equipment? How did it work in practical terms? How did it work in visual terms?

The presentation in action

Did the set-up go smoothly? Did the presenter look and sound effective when presenting? Could everyone hear? If a team effort, were introductions and handovers made effectively and smoothly? Did the team presentation 'gel'?

Gaining feedback

You can't rely solely on your own impressions for accurate feedback although these are important as we'll see in a minute. For one thing, you may have been so nervous or so focused that the whole event passed by in a bit of a blur, and your main feeling at the end was one of sheer relief!

So you need to ask your colleagues, and if possible your audience, what they felt about your performance. There are a number of ways of doing this.

Immediate feedback

As soon as you have time after the presentation, jot down your first impressions. This could be done in the car park before leaving the venue, on the train going home, or as soon as you reach your desk. The important thing is to do it quickly, before you forget, using a form as suggested earlier. No matter how many urgent messages are waiting for you, note down your impressions first, and ask any colleagues presenting to do the same. The result can be used for more in-depth analysis later.

Debriefing meeting

This is more relevant to team presentations, but can be held with anyone who was involved in helping you, even if they weren't there on the big day. Draw up an agenda based on the list above, detailing those areas you want to cover, and make sure everyone brings the notes they made immediately after the presentation. Just as a brainstorming session will have helped you in the creation of a presentation, a formal post-presentation brainstorm will help deconstruct the event piece by piece and analyze effectively. Of course, during such a meeting you may find that each individual has a very different impression of what happened, which may give rise to lively discussion.

The feedback form

Placed prominently in any handouts, a feedback form is a useful way of generating comments on your presentation. It's often used if you have been presenting material which has to be 'understood': it's not appropriate for formal presentations, where the audience has invited you, business pitches, or presentations to the board, for example. Make reference to the form within your presentation, give your audience time to complete it at the end, and provide a box into which the forms can be dropped. Giving your audience the chance to remain anonymous will help increase returns.

The Old Town Business Club has a standard form they use for each of their evening presentations. Here's the one they handed out to the delegates who attended Tom Collins's presentation:

Date:	27/1/99
Presentation:	Using the Internet for Business
Presenter:	Tom Collins, Information for Business

Thank you for coming along to this evening's presentation, which is one of a series run by the Old Town Business Club. We are always keen to gain feedback from delegates, as this helps us plan future events and makes sure our presentation programme continues to be of the highest standard possible. To help us, we would be grateful if you could complete this feedback form and hand it in at the end of the presentation.

Overall, did the presentation meet your expectations?

If not, why not?

How would you describe the presenter's style?

Was his presentation well structured and logical?

Did visual aids contribute effectively to the presentation? Were they clear and easy to see?

Was any handout material useful?

Was the timing given to the presentation accurate and adequate?

Were question and answer sessions handled effectively?

Are there any further comments you would like to add?

Informal questioning

If your audience comprises work colleagues, then it will be fairly easy to request feedback from them, either formally (using a version of the feedback form outlined above) or informally by talking to a sample of those who attended. You could even prime a colleague or friendly audience member in advance. They'll be watching even more attentively, and will be ready with interesting comments after the event.

Formal request for a feedback meeting

Not all presentation audiences will want to provide feedback. Audiences which plan to make a serious decision based on what they hear, perhaps concerning contracts, promotions or business development plans, will not want to be chased for their opinion on your delivery style: even more so when presenting alongside competing teams. In these situations you may find your audience will hold their cards very close to their chests indeed: the audience will consider its final decision to be criticism or accolade enough.

Such situations can give rise to very confusing results. What you perceived to be an enthusiastically received, well-delivered presentation fails to gain you the business you expected, and you simply can't tell why. In such situations, it's even more important to try to get some form of feedback from your audience. It might be that your prices were simply uncompetitive or something significant had changed and you hadn't been informed. If you don't ask, you'll never know, and risk undermining your confidence when it comes to planning your next important presentation.

Within this context, a realistic strategy is to keep in touch with your main contact within the 'host' organization and try to arrange a time to discuss your presentation formally, by telephone, meeting, or even an exchange of letters. Use your own judgement, knowledge of your relationship with your contact and an appreciation of how busy he or she is to choose the best option. The worst thing he or she can say is 'no': but by asking it will show that you are keen to learn from experience, and anxious to do well. Most people in business appreciate that improvements can only be made if accurate feedback is provided.

Even if your presentation has been successful in a business sense – you've won the contract, or prompted the right decision – formal feedback can still yield interesting and useful information, especially if you can find out why your competitors failed.

Video the presentation

In some situations, for example larger presentations, seminars or training presentations, you could video the whole event and replay it afterwards to a group of colleagues in order to judge your performance. This is especially useful if you need to assess a presentation which you will be delivering a number of times.

What next?

Once you've obtained all this valuable information, it's important not simply to file it away and forget about it. You need to make sure that the next presentation builds on and makes the most of all this hard-won knowledge.

Translating feedback into positive action can be done in a number of ways.

Create a 'Best Practice Manual'

Start to build up a central resource which catalogues good advice on presentation techniques, as well as hints and tips on what to avoid. Store it electronically for Intranet access, or keep it in a simple ring binder and add new information over time. Identifying best practice is a first step towards establishing a 'house style': a formalized set of presentation guidelines which everyone in your organization can follow. A house style makes presentation preparation easier and also results in a more coherent image for your organization in general. Include good advice gained from other sources, such as magazine articles, presentations other colleagues have delivered successfully (or otherwise), notes from training courses and so on.

Brush up skills

If a lack of confidence or skill in a certain area has been identified, make sure training is arranged before the next major presentation. It may not simply be lack of experience that has caused a problem: a team or individual that has been presenting for a long time may also need a refresher course to help correct bad habits and introduce new ideas.

You may have felt under-rehearsed: if so, note this in the Best Practice Manual and try to identify a minimum number of rehearsals for each type of presentation your organization usually delivers.

Improve information resources

If you are presenting regularly and have had to spend considerable time researching background information, then investing in more sources of information may be worthwhile, and your feedback mechanisms will indicate when the time has come to investigate this matter. Look at the suggestions made in Chapter 2, such as an on-line information service or business membership of a major library.

Upgrade presentation equipment

If you have borrowed yet another unreliable OHP, or been forced to use a rackety, old-fashioned slide projector, then you may need to consider investing in equipment of your own. You don't need to spend a great deal of money (although you most certainly could if you wanted to), but it's probably worth spending a decent sum if the equipment you buy is to last you, reliably, through many presentations. Alternatively, investigate reputable hire shops that can provide more reliable equipment next time you need it.

Venue and supplier records

Depending upon the complexity of the presentation, you may have used a number of suppliers for venue hire, catering, equipment hire, transport, accommodation and so on. A database of reliable suppliers is often a godsend to any organizer, and will save considerable time when next planning a presentation. Likewise, make a note of any supplier that let you down, or of any venue that proved less hospitable than it could have been. Brochures from possible future suppliers, sent on spec, could also be housed in the same file but make a note that they are as yet untried, and don't use them for your most important presentations until you are sure they are good enough.

A new wardrobe?

If you felt your personal appearance let you down, then take time – away from the pressure of an imminent presentation – to buy a new outfit. Sales are becoming a regular event in every high street, so don't feel you have to spend a small fortune. It may just be that one item – a jacket or skirt – needs replacing, or perhaps a completely new look is needed to boost flagging confidence.

And finally . . .

It is important to make the most of the experience you have gained each time you present, no matter how informal or relatively unplanned the presentation may have been. As we said right at the beginning of the book, good presentations rely on good planning, and the combined experience of many presentations can help reduce your planning time significantly. And as a result, even if you are asked to present this very afternoon, you will be able to deliver a confident, effective presentation which will achieve its objectives – and even be an enjoyable experience.

Summary

■ As soon as you have delivered your presentation, analyze your performance using as many different methods as possible.

■ Analyze the planning, content and delivery of your presentation.

■ Translate your resulting analysis into practical actions which can benefit your next presentation and those of your colleagues.

Do it yourself

Draft your own internal feedback form and use it to analyze the next presentation you attend, even if it's simply watching a lecture on TV.

Section Two
PRESENTER'S CHECKLISTS

PRESENTER'S CHECKLISTS

Most of the information given in Section One is relevant to all presentation scenarios: this section brings together some of the essential, practical points, grouping them according to specific presentation contexts.

Presenting to an external audience, or one which has invited you to present

- Keep in close touch with the organizer in order to make sure everything stays according to the initial brief.
- Be precise when establishing the nature of the venue, especially if you can't visit it before you present. Double-check all details a day or two before you arrive.
- If you're on your own, make sure you have a stand-in if necessary.
- Personal presentation is even more important because you are representing your organization as well as yourself.
- If you have selected, or are in control of, the venue make sure it looks its best.
- OHP, 35 mm slides or multimedia presentations give the most professional results.
- If travelling to present, make sure you allow yourself enough time to set up properly.
- If travelling away from the office, make sure you know exactly where you're going.
- If your external audience is geographically widespread, or the presentation may be one of longer term interest, consider presenting on CD, video or over the Internet.
- Try to gain feedback formally, either by meeting, telephone or exchange of letters.

Presenting to colleagues, in-house

- If booking meeting rooms or shared equipment, make sure it isn't 'borrowed' before the big day.
- Identify any office politics which may influence the way you present.
- A level of informality is more acceptable and may make your audience feel more relaxed.
- Prime a colleague to give you specific feedback after the event.

Presenting one-to-one, or to a small group

- Use of notes or *aides-mémoires* can look odd. Use your visual aids as prompts, or jot down a few key points on a piece of paper, kept in a formal document wallet.
- Flip charts, whiteboards, portfolios or laptops are good presentation options (portfolios and laptops for groups of five or less).

Team presentations

- Choose co-presenters with care: you'll need to field a good mix of subject knowledge and presentational ability.
- Establish responsibilities early on in the planning procedure.
- Choose a project manager to plan the presentation, and a leader to 'host' the event: these need not be the same person.
- You'll need more rehearsal time, so book this into diaries well in advance.
- Practise presenting in a similar style, although avoid appearing identical.
- Script handovers and learn them by heart.
- Decide in advance what each team member is going to wear, to avoid embarrassing duplication or colour clashes.
- Make sure everyone has been properly introduced before you start.

Seat your team to the left of any screen, and avoid crossing any display equipment during handovers.

Look alert and interested when not presenting.

If you need to record information on a flip chart, make sure it's positioned so that left- and right-handed team members can write on it easily.

Nominate one team member to host the question and answer session.

Make sure questions are distributed evenly across all members of the team.

Presenting to a large audience

Depending upon the formality of the occasion, a speech – read out verbatim – is more acceptable in this context.

■ Practise speaking in a larger venue, to judge the pitch and tone of your voice correctly. Remember that your voice will sound different when the venue is full.

If using visual display equipment, make sure it has sufficient 'throw': that it will project an image large enough for all audience members to see, and one which remains clear and bright.

Make sure all sections of the audience can hear you when you speak and can hear each other when they ask questions. Additional amplification may be needed, both on the platform and in the auditorium.

CD, Internet and video presentations are good alternatives when presenting to large groups of people.

FURTHER READING

For information on some of the more specific points covered in this book, consult the following:

Gabay, J. Jonathan, 1996, *Teach Yourself Copywriting*. London: Hodder and Stoughton

Mason, Roger, 1996, *Teach Yourself Speaking on Special Occasions*. London: Hodder and Stoughton

Looker, Terry and Olga Gregson, 1997, *Teach Yourself Managing Stress*. London: Hodder and Stoughton

A wide range of reference books is available to help clarify points of grammar and check spelling: the following are some of the best known. Look for the most recent editions when you go to your local bookshop:

Collins Dictionary of the English Language. London: Collins

The Oxford Dictionary for Writers and Editors. Oxford: Clarendon Press

The Oxford Minidictionary of Spelling and Word Division. Oxford: Clarendon Press

ACKNOWLEDGEMENTS

The survey referred to in our Introduction was from *Men's Health*, April 1998.

Every effort has been made to contact the holders of copyright material but if any have been inadvertently overlooked, the Publisher will be pleased to make the necessary alterations at the first opportunity.

USEFUL ADDRESSES

If you are in any doubt about copyright, the following organizations may be able to help you:

The Patent Office
25 Southampton Buildings
Chancery Lane
London WC2 1AY
Tel: 0171 438 4778
Fax: 0171 438 4780
www.patent.gov.uk

The Copyright Licensing Agency Ltd
90 Tottenham Court Road
London WIP 0LP
Tel: 0171 436 5931
Fax: 0171 436 3986
www.cla.co.uk

Society of Authors
84 Drayton Gardens
London SW10 9SB

INDEX

aides-mémoires
  notes 85
  presenting without 86
  scripts 83
audience
  assessing knowledge 16, 73
  changing size 49
  feedback 153
  participation 74
  predicting expectations 18
  surveying 76
audience types
  bored 19
  hostile 19
  reserved 19
  supportive 19
audio, use of 114
audio-visual equipment
  35mm slide projector 131
  failure of 46
  flipchart 124
  LCD projection panel 128, 134
  overhead projector (OHP) 127
  PC/multimedia technology 133
  planning ahead 31
  portfolio 126
  tape recorder 114
  upgrading 158
  VCR 115
  whiteboard 124

background research 57
back-up presentation 35

'best practice' manual 157
body language 93
brainstorming 52
brief, the 7
  responding to 10
  rejecting 16
  writing your own 15
budgeting 41

CD presentations 137
communication skills 83
computers
  CD, Internet and Intranet
    presentations 137
  large-screen PCs 134
  LCD projection panels 128, 134
  LCD and DLP projectors 134
  multi-media presentations 133
  presentation software 115
contingency planning 46
copyright 62
creative thinking 54
  dropped dictionary 56
  mind mapping 55
credentials presentation 73

deadlines
  meeting the impossible 44
  respecting 21
discussion sessions 78

entertaining
  assessing the venue 31

planning ahead 32
  setting up 143
eye contact 95

feedback, audience 153
  debriefing 154
  feedback form 154
  formal 156
  informal 155
  video 156
furniture
  assessing needs 30
  last minute changes 48
  setting up 142

games 75, 77
good or bad news, presenting 71
grammar 120

handout material
  core material 36
  emergency 45
  follow-on 37
  planning 36
  supportive material 36
  when to give out 148
hidden agenda 16

illustrations (for visual aids)
  copyright 63
  figures and diagrams 113
  photos 113
  pictures 113
  words 112
Internet and Intranet presentations 137
introductions 75, 145

laser pointer 137
leaving the venue 150

media, presenting to 71
multi-media presentations 133

personal presentation 101
  colour analysis 107
  grooming 106
  presentation wardrobe 108
  what to wear when 102
planning timetable 27
post-presentation analysis 152
  actions resulting from 157
  feedback 153
  planning for 152
presentation box 144
presentation content
  creative process 51
  managing and writing 64
  planning 33
  reviewing drafts 35
  starting and ending 66, 75
presentation types
  informative 3, 4
  instructive 3, 4
  one to one 164
  persuasive 3
  standard/pre-prepared 45, 73, 127
  team 20, 34, 96, 97, 164
  to a large audience 165
  to an external audience 163
  to colleagues 164
presenters
  booking 28
  understudies 29, 49
press launch 71
project management
  project manager 26
  scheduling activities 42
props 80

questions and answers
  aggressive questioners 71, 101
  answering difficult questions 99
  managing 98
  when to place 80

rehearsals 39, 89
  with audio-visual equipment 138
relaxation 89
  eating and drinking 90
  techniques 90
remembering names and faces 146
role play 79

setting up 141
  checklist 142
  dressing the set 143
statistics, presenting 69, 113
strategic planning 7, 21
summaries, presenting 69
supportive material
  improving resources 157
  in-house archive 62
  qualitative market research 60
  sources of information 57, 58
  use of 57

team presentations 164
  choosing team members 20
  handovers 96
  personal presentation 105
  seating 97
  writing content 34
third-party approval 34
training presentations 72

training, professional 39, 138
  post-presentation 157
travelling to present
  planning ahead 33
  running late 46

venue
  assessment 29, 158
  booking 27
  leaving 150
  signposting 47
  unexpected changes 46
video
  clips (as content) 114
  presentations 137
  use for feedback 156
  use for rehearsals
    (body language) 94
visual aids
  at short notice 44
  creating 111
  design and style 116
  planning ahead 35
  presenting information visually 119
  setting up 143
voice control 91

workshops 79